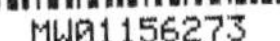

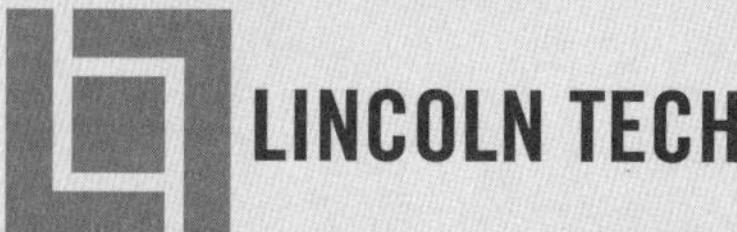

Lincoln Technical Institute

Tasksheet Manual

VOLUME 2

JONES & BARTLETT
LEARNING

World Headquarters
Jones & Bartlett Learning
5 Wall Street
Burlington, MA 01803
978-443-5000
info@jblearning.com
www.jblearning.com

Jones & Bartlett Learning books and products are available through most bookstores and online booksellers. To contact Jones & Bartlett Learning directly, call 800-832-0034, fax 978-443-8000, or visit our website, www.jblearning.com.

Substantial discounts on bulk quantities of Jones & Bartlett Learning publications are available to corporations, professional associations, and other qualified organizations. For details and specific discount information, contact the special sales department at Jones & Bartlett Learning via the above contact information or send an email to specialsales@jblearning.com.

978-1284-16482-4

Production Credits

General Manager: Kimberly Brophy
VP, Product Development: Christine Emerton
Content Services Manager: Kevin Murphy
Product Manager: Jesse Mitchell
Editorial Assistant: Jessica Sturtevant
Senior Vendor Manager: Sara Kelly
Marketing Manager: Amanda Banner
Manufacturing and Inventory Control Supervisor: Amy Bacus
Composition and Project Management: Integra Software Services Pvt. Ltd.
Cover Design: Scott Moden
Director of Rights & Media: Joanna Gallant
Rights & Media Specialist: Robert Boder
Media Development Editor: Shannon Sheehan
Cover Image (Title Page): © Umberto Shtanzman/Shutterstock
Printing and Binding: McNaughton & Gunn
Cover Printing: McNaughton & Gunn

Library of Congress Cataloging-in-Publication Data

6048

Printed in the United States of America

22 21 20 10 9 8 7 6 5 4

Contents

▶ TASK Research vehicle service information including fluid type, vehicle service history, service precautions, and technical service bulletins.

MAST 4A1

Time off________

Time on________

Total time________

CDX Tasksheet Number: C166

1. **Using the VIN for identification, use the appropriate source to access the vehicle's service history in relation to prior related suspension and steering system work or customer concerns.**
    a. **List any related steering and suspension system repairs/concerns and their dates:**

2. **Using the VIN for identification, access any relevant technical service bulletins for the particular vehicle you are working on in relation to steering and suspension updates or other service issues.**
    a. **List any steering and suspension system-related service bulletins and their titles:**

3. **Research the type of front and rear suspension used on this vehicle and list here:**

4. **Research the type of steering system used on this vehicle and list here:**

5. **Research the type of steering fluid required for this vehicle and list it here:**

6. **Have your supervisor/instructor verify satisfactory completion of this procedure, any observations found, and any necessary action(s) recommended.**

Performance Rating

CDX Tasksheet Number: C166

☐	☐	☐	☐	☐
0	1	2	3	4

Supervisor/instructor signature ______________________ Date ____________

▶ TASK Identify and interpret suspension and steering system concerns; determine needed action.

MAST 4A2

Time off________

Time on________

Total time________

CDX Tasksheet Number: C851

1. **List the customer concern:**

2. **Research the particular concern in the appropriate service information.**
   a. **List the possible causes:**

3. **Inspect the steering and suspension system to determine the cause of the concern. List the steps you took to determine the fault:**

4. **List the cause of the concern:**

5. **List the necessary action(s) to correct this fault:**

6. **Have your supervisor/instructor verify satisfactory completion of this procedure, any observations found, and any necessary action(s) recommended.**

Performance Rating

CDX Tasksheet Number: C851

☐	☐	☐	☐	☐
0	1	2	3	4

Supervisor/instructor signature ________________ Date ________

▶ TASK Demonstrate the use of the three Cs (concern, cause, correction). **Additional Task**

Time off________

Time on________

Total time________

CDX Tasksheet Number: N/A

1. **Using the following scenario, write up the three Cs as listed on most repair orders. Assume that the customer authorized the recommended repairs.**

A vehicle is brought to your shop with a steering or suspension concern. The customer tells you that the vehicle has been pulling to the right ever since he hit a big pothole on a recent trip. The vehicle also has a vibration that is very noticeable when driving and is getting worse. He would like an estimate before the end of the day, because he will be leaving on a two-week vacation in the morning, and he would like the vehicle repaired while he is away. You test-drive the vehicle to verify the concerns, pull the vehicle up on the alignment hoist, and find the following:

   a. **The tires are only a few months old, but the right front tire has broken belts as evidenced by the bulge in one edge.**
   b. **The right front wheel has a bent flange.**
   c. **The wheel alignment machine shows improper toe-out on turns that, upon further inspection, are shown to be caused by a bent right front steering arm on the steering knuckle.**
   d. **The rear struts are excessively worn and don't dampen like they should.**
   e. **The vehicle is about 1000 miles past its scheduled oil and filter change.**
   f. **The serpentine belt is showing excessive wear.**

> **NOTE** Ask your instructor if you should use the shop's repair order to complete this task, or the three Cs listed here.

2. **Concern/complaint:**

3. **Cause:**

4. **Correction:**

5. **Other recommended service:**

6. **Have your supervisor/instructor verify satisfactory completion of this procedure, any observations found, and any necessary action(s) recommended.**

Performance Rating

CDX Tasksheet Number: N/A

0	1	2	3	4

Supervisor/instructor signature ______________________ Date ________

▶ TASK Inspect tire condition; identify tire wear patterns; check for correct size, application (load and speed ratings), and air pressure as listed on the tire information placard/label.

Time off________

Time on________

Total time________

CDX Tasksheet Number: C619

1. **Research tread wear patterns in the appropriate information.**

2. **Research the following tire specifications on the vehicle's tire decal and on the sidewall of the tire itself:**

   a. **Tire decal (usually located on the vehicle door, door pillar, or glove box lid):**
   Recommended tire designation: ________
   Maximum load on front axle: ________ **lb/kg**
   Maximum load on rear axle: ________ **lb/kg**
   Required tire speed rating: ________
   Maximum speed for this rating: ________ **mph/kph**
   Recommended tire pressure: Front: ________ **psi/kPa**
   Rear: ________ **psi/kPa**

   b. **Information on sidewall of tire:**
   Tire designation: ________
   Maximum load: ________ **lb/kg**
   Speed rating: ________ **Speed tire is safe for:** ________ **mph/kph**
   Maximum tire pressure: ________ **psi/kPa**
   Tread wear rating: ________
   Traction rating: ________
   Temperature rating: ________
   DOT date of manufacture code: ________ **Age of tire today:** ___ **(yrs/mos)**

3. **On the most-worn tire, measure the tread depth across the tire tread and list your measurements below:**

   a. **Tread depth (inside of tread):** ________ **in/mm**
   b. **Tread depth (center of tread):** ________ **in/mm**
   c. **Tread depth (outside of tread):** ________ **in/mm**

4. **Check to make sure there are no exposed steel cords. Carefully run your hand across the tread and feel for a feathered condition. Also, run your hand in line with the tread to feel for lumps and bulges.**

   a. **Is the tire feathered? Yes:** ________ **No:** ________
   b. **Are there any bulges? Yes:** ________ **No:** ________

5. **Based on your observations and measurements, determine what, if any, wear patterns exist and list them here:**

6. **Measure the pressure in the tire(s) and record it here:** ________ **psi/kPa**

7. **If the tire is not at the correct pressure, increase or decrease pressure.**
   a. **Record final pressure: ________________ psi/kPa**

8. **Determine any necessary action(s):**

9. **Have your supervisor/instructor verify satisfactory completion of this procedure, any observations found, and any necessary action(s) recommended.**

Performance Rating

CDX Tasksheet Number: C619

☐	☐	☐	☐	☐
0	1	2	3	4

Supervisor/instructor signature ________________________ Date ____________

▶ TASK Rotate tires according to manufacturer's recommendations including vehicles equipped with tire pressure monitoring systems (TPMS).

MAST
4F3

Time off__________

Time on__________

Total time__________

CDX Tasksheet Number: C222

1. **Research the following specifications in the appropriate service information.**

> **NOTE** Vehicles equipped with a tire pressure monitoring system (TPMS) may need the system reset after rotating the tires. Verify that you have all the necessary tools and manufacturer's procedure prior to removing the wheels on these vehicles.

   a. **Is this vehicle equipped with TPMS? Yes: __________ No: __________**
      i. **If yes, do you have the specified tools and procedures to reset the TPMS system? Yes: __________ No: __________**
   b. **Lug nut torque: ______________ ft-lb/N·m**
   c. **Manufacturer's recommended tire rotation pattern. Draw diagram below.**

   d. **Manufacturer's recommended lug nut torque sequence. Draw diagram below.**

2. **Remove the wheel/tire assemblies from the vehicle.**

> **NOTE** When removing hubcaps and wheels, please store them in such a manner so as not to damage the visible side of the hubcap or wheel. Laying them face down will cause them to become scratched and damaged. Also, store the lug nuts so they will not get lost or kicked.

3. **Have your supervisor/instructor verify removal.**
   Supervisor's/instructor's initials: __________

4. **Rotate the tires according to the manufacturer's recommendation. As part of this procedure, check the tire pressure. If a tire is found to be under-inflated, check the tire for a leak. If a leak is found, notify your supervisor/instructor for further directions. Also, inspect each tire for nails or other foreign objects. Notify your supervisor/instructor if a problem is found. List your observations:**

5. **Torque the lug nuts to manufacturer's specifications in the specified sequence.**
   a. **Record torque: ____________________ ft-lbs/N·m**

6. **Reset TPMS if necessary. Follow manufacturer's procedure.**

7. **Reinstall hubcaps, if equipped. Make sure they are fully seated to prevent them from falling off while driving. If in doubt, ask your supervisor/instructor.**

8. **Have your supervisor/instructor verify satisfactory completion of this procedure, any observations found, and any necessary action(s) recommended.**

Performance Rating

CDX Tasksheet Number: C222

☐	☐	☐	☐	☐
0	1	2	3	4

Supervisor/instructor signature ______________________________ Date ____________

TASK Dismount, inspect, and remount tire on wheel; balance wheel and tire assembly.

MAST 4F6

Time off________

Time on________

Total time________

CDX Tasksheet Number: C620

NOTE Verify that this wheel is NOT equipped with TPMS.

1. **List the customer concern, if any:**

2. **Prepare the vehicle and remove the wheel concerned.**

3. **Inspect the outer surface of the entire wheel and tire assembly. List your observations:**

4. **Using the correct procedure, dismount the tire from the wheel.**

5. **Inspect the inside of the tire, the tire bead, the inside of the rim, and the valve stem. List your observations:**

6. **Have your supervisor/instructor verify removal.**
   Supervisor's/instructor's initials: ________

7. **Remount tire on the wheel using the correct equipment and procedure.**

8. **Balance wheel and tire assembly (static and dynamic) and draw a diagram of the position and size of the weights:**

9. **Determine any necessary action(s):**

10. **Have your supervisor/instructor verify satisfactory completion of this procedure, any observations found, and any necessary action(s) recommended.**

Performance Rating

CDX Tasksheet Number: C620

0	1	2	3	4
☐	☐	☐	☐	☐

Supervisor/instructor signature ______________________ Date ________

▶ TASK Demonstrate knowledge of steps required to remove and replace sensors in a tire pressure monitoring system (TPMS) including relearn procedure.

MAST 4F11

Time off__________

Time on__________

Total time__________

CDX Tasksheet Number: C936

1. **Research the procedure for replacing TPMS sensors on at least 3 vehicles (1 domestic car, 1 imported car, and 1 all-wheel drive vehicle) in the appropriate service information.**
   a. **Vehicle year, make, and model:** ________________________
      i. **Summarize the steps to replace the TPMS sensor:**

      ii. **List any precautions when replacing the TPMS sensor:**

      iii. **List the procedure to calibrate or relearn the TPMS system:**

   b. **Vehicle year, make, and model:** ________________________
      i. **Summarize the steps to replace the TPMS sensor:**

      ii. **List any precautions when replacing the TPMS sensor:**

iii. List the procedure to calibrate or relearn the TPMS system:

c. Vehicle year, make, and model: ___________

i. Summarize the steps to replace the TPMS sensor:

ii. List any precautions when replacing the TPMS sensor:

iii. List the procedure to calibrate or relearn the TPMS system:

2. Have your supervisor/instructor verify satisfactory completion of this procedure, any observations found, and any necessary action(s) recommended.

Performance Rating
CDX Tasksheet Number: C936
0
1
2
3
4
Supervisor/instructor signature
Date

▶ TASK Dismount, inspect, and remount tire on wheel equipped with tire pressure monitoring system sensor.

MAST 4F7

Time off________

Time on________

Total time________

CDX Tasksheet Number: C621

Vehicle used for this activity:

Year ____________ Make ________________________ Model ________________________

Odometer ____________________ VIN ____

1. **List the customer concern, if any:**

2. **Research the following in the appropriate service information:**
   a. **Tire removal/installation on TPMS-equipped vehicles. List the proper positioning of the wheel on the tire machine when removing the tire:**

   b. **TPMS maintenance needs and service. List any maintenance that can be performed on the TPMS sensors:**

   c. **TPMS reset procedure, if necessary. List the steps to reset the TPMS sensors:**

3. **Prepare the vehicle and remove the wheel concerned.**

4. **Inspect the outer surface of the entire wheel and tire assembly. List your observations:**

5. **Using the correct procedure, dismount the tire from the wheel. Be careful not to damage the TPMS sensor.**

6. **Inspect the inside of the tire, the tire bead, the inside of the rim, the valve stem, and the TPMS sensor. List your observations:**

7. **Have your supervisor/instructor verify removal.**
   Supervisor's/instructor's initials: ______________________

8. **Perform any needed maintenance/service on the TPMS system.**
   List your actions:

9. **Remount tire on wheel using the correct equipment and procedure. Be careful not to damage the TPMS sensor.**

10. **Balance wheel and tire assembly, if necessary, and draw a diagram of the position and size of the weights:**

11. **Reinstall wheel/tire assembly on the vehicle and torque lug nuts to the proper torque in the proper sequence.**

12. **If necessary, reset the TPMS according to the specified procedure. List your observations:**

13. **Determine any necessary action(s):**

14. **Have your supervisor/instructor verify satisfactory completion of this procedure, any observations found, and any necessary action(s) recommended.**

Performance Rating

CDX Tasksheet Number: C621

☐	☐	☐	☐	☐
0	1	2	3	4

Supervisor/instructor signature _______________ Date _______________

▶ TASK Diagnose wheel/tire vibration, shimmy, and noise; determine needed action.

MAST 4F2

Time off________

Time on________

Total time________

CDX Tasksheet Number: C855

Vehicle used for this activity:

Year ____________ Make __________________________ Model __________________________

Odometer ____________________ VIN ____

1. **List the wheel/tire-related customer concern(s):**

2. **Research the concern in the appropriate service information and any technical service bulletins that may apply.**
    a. **List any applicable service bulletins:**
    b. **List or print off and attach to this sheet the procedure for diagnosing the concern:**

3. **With the supervisor's/instructor's permission, test-drive the vehicle. Listen and feel for any unusual noises and vibrations. List your observations:**

4. **Using the recommended procedure, inspect and diagnose any vibration, shimmy, or noise concerns. List your tests and results here:**

5. **List the cause of the concern:**

6. **Determine any necessary action(s) to correct the fault:**

7. **Have your supervisor/instructor verify satisfactory completion of this procedure, any observations found, and any necessary action(s) recommended.**

Performance Rating

CDX Tasksheet Number: C855

0	1	2	3	4
☐	☐	☐	☐	☐

Supervisor/instructor signature ______________________ Date ________

▶ TASK Diagnose tire pull problems; determine needed action.

MAST 4F5

Time off________

Time on________

Total time________

CDX Tasksheet Number: C796

Vehicle used for this activity:

Year ____________ Make ____________________ Model ____________________

Odometer ____________________ VIN ____

1. **List the tire pull-related customer concern(s):**

2. **Research the configuration of this vehicle in the appropriate service information and any technical service bulletins that may apply.**
   a. **List any applicable service bulletins and their titles:**

   b. **List or print off and attach to this sheet the procedure for diagnosing the concern:**

3. **With the supervisor's/instructor's permission, test-drive the vehicle. Check for any tire pull problems. List your observations:**

4. **Using the recommended procedure, inspect and diagnose any tire pull problems. List your tests and results here:**

5. **List the cause of the concern:**

6. Determine any necessary action(s) to correct the fault:

7. Have your supervisor/instructor verify satisfactory completion of this procedure, any observations found, and any necessary action(s) recommended.

Performance Rating

CDX Tasksheet Number: C796

0	1	2	3	4

Supervisor/instructor signature _______________ Date _______

▶ TASK Inspect tire and wheel assembly for air loss; perform needed action.

Time off__________

Time on__________

Total time__________

CDX Tasksheet Number: C580

1. **Research the following specifications in the appropriate service information.**
   a. **Lug nut torque: __________ ft-lb/N·m**
   b. **Is this vehicle equipped with TPMS? Yes: ________ No: ________**
   c. **If yes, do you have the specified tools and procedures to reset the TPMS system? Yes: ________ No: ________**

2. **Remove wheel/tire assembly from vehicle and check it for any leaks using soapy water or a dunk tank. List your observations:**

NOTE When removing hubcaps and wheels, please store them in such a manner as not to damage the visible side of the hubcap or wheel. Laying them face down will cause them to become scratched and damaged. Also store the lug nuts so they will not get lost or kicked.

3. **Mark the position of all wheel weights and the valve stem on the tire with a tire crayon. This is so you can reinstall the tire and weights on the wheel in the same position so rebalancing is unnecessary.**

4. **Using the correct procedure, dismount the tire from the wheel. Be careful not to damage the TPMS, if equipped.**

5. **Inspect the wheel and tire for any damage, rust, or other defects and list them here:**

6. **Are the defects repairable? Yes: ________ No: ________**

7. **Have your supervisor/instructor verify your observations, and ask permission to make any repairs. Supervisor's/instructor initials: __________**

8. **With supervisor/instructor approval, repair all defects found.**

NOTE If the tire has a leak that can be repaired with an integrated plug-patch or internal patch, skip ahead to task C552: Repair tire following vehicle manufacturer approved procedure, and return here once the task has been completed.

9. **Remount the tire on the wheel, positioning the tire and weights in their original positions on the wheel to restore existing tire balance.**

10. **Recheck the wheel/tire assembly for leaks. If there are none, reinstall it on the vehicle and torque the lug nuts to the proper specification and in the proper sequence.**

11. **Have your supervisor/instructor verify satisfactory completion of this procedure, any observations found, and any necessary action(s) recommended.**

Performance Rating

CDX Tasksheet Number: C580

0	1	2	3	4
☐	☐	☐	☐	☐

Supervisor/instructor signature ________________________ Date __________

▶ TASK Repair tire following vehicle manufacturer approved procedure.

MAST 4F9

Time off________

Time on________

Total time________

CDX Tasksheet Number: C552

1. **Inspect the tire for remaining tread life and ensure that any repair undertaken will meet all legislative requirements.**
    a. **Measure the minimum tread depth: ________________ in/mm**
    b. **Is the tread depth above the legal limit? Yes: __________ No: __________**
    c. **Is the hole within the repairable zone of the tread? Yes: __________ No: __________**
    d. **Is the diameter of the hole within patching limits? Yes: __________ No: __________**
    e. **What type of internal patch are you using? Standard internal patch: __________ Integrated plug patch: __________**

2. **Using a recommended method, prepare the tire for repair, (perform all steps except applying glue and the patch). List your steps and observations here:**

3. **Have your instructor verify the proper preparation for the patch. Supervisor's/instructor initials: ________________**

4. **Determine any necessary action(s), and undertake the repair by applying the glue and patch in accordance with the manufacturer's recommendations and process (most tire patch glues MUST be allowed to fully dry before applying the patch).**

5. **Have your supervisor/instructor verify satisfactory completion of this procedure, any observations found, and any necessary action(s) recommended.**

Performance Rating

CDX Tasksheet Number: C552

☐	☐	☐	☐	☐
0	1	2	3	4

Supervisor/instructor signature ________________________ Date __________

▶ TASK Measure wheel, tire, axle flange, and hub runout; determine needed action.

MAST 4F4

Time off________

Time on________

Total time________

CDX Tasksheet Number: C701

Vehicle used for this activity:

Year ________ Make ________ Model ________

Odometer ________ VIN ________

1. **List the customer concern; if applicable:**

2. **Research the procedure for measuring tire, wheel, and hub runout in the appropriate service information. List the following specifications:**

   a. **Tire pressure: ________ psi/kPa**
   b. **Tire designation: ________**
   c. **Maximum tire runout: ________ in/mm**
   d. **Maximum wheel runout: ________ in/mm**
   e. **Maximum axle flange/hub runout: ________ in/mm**

3. **Check and adjust the tire pressures according to specifications.**

4. **Inspect each tire and list its designation:**

   a. **LF tire: ________**
   b. **RF tire: ________**
   c. **RR tire: ________**
   d. **LR tire: ________**
   e. **Does each tire meet the manufacturer's recommendations?**
      Yes: ________ No: ________

5. **Properly raise the front of the vehicle and support it securely.**

6. **Following the manufacturer's procedure, measure runout of the following:**

   a. **LF tire: ________ in/mm**
   b. **RF tire: ________ in/mm**
   c. **LF wheel: ________ in/mm**
   d. **RF wheel: ________ in/mm**
   e. **LF hub: ________ in/mm**
   f. **RF hub: ________ in/mm**

7. **Determine any necessary action(s):**

8. **Have your supervisor/instructor verify satisfactory completion of this procedure, any observations found, and any necessary action(s) recommended.**

Performance Rating

CDX Tasksheet Number: C701

□	□	□	□	□
0	1	2	3	4

Supervisor/instructor signature ______________________ Date ____________

▶ TASK Identify indirect and direct tire pressure monitoring system (TPMS); calibrate system; verify operation of instrument panel lamps.

MAST
4F10

Time off________

Time on________

Total time________

CDX Tasksheet Number: C937

Vehicle used for this activity:

Year ____________ Make ____________________ Model ____________________

Odometer ____________________ VIN ______________________________

1. **Research the TPMS system in the appropriate service information.**
   a. **Choose the type of TMPS system: Indirect: ________ Direct: ________**
   b. **List or print off and attach to this sheet the process for calibrating the TPMS system:**
   c. **List how the instrument panel warning lamps should behave if the system is operating normally:**
   d. **List how the instrument panel warning lamps should behave if the system is NOT operating normally:**

2. **Describe how an indirect TPMS system detects a tire with low tire pressure:**

3. **Describe how a direct TPMS system detects a tire with low tire pressure:**

4. **Check the operation of the TPMS warning lamp and list your observations:**

5. **Swap the two front-wheel assemblies and calibrate the TPMS system in accordance with the manufacturer's instructions. List your steps and observations here:**

6. **Have your supervisor/instructor verify satisfactory completion of this procedure, any observations found, and any necessary action(s) recommended.**

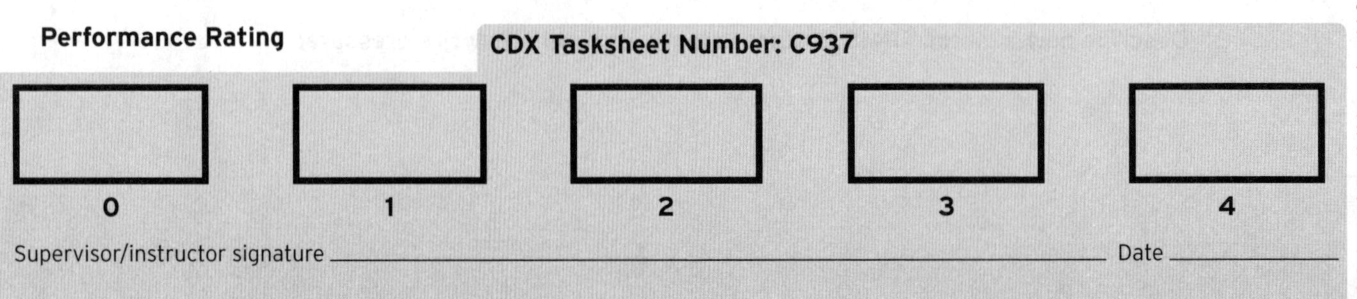

Performance Rating

CDX Tasksheet Number: C937

0 1 2 3 4

Supervisor/instructor signature ______________________ Date __________

TASK Describe the function of suspension and steering control systems and components (i.e. active suspension and stability control).

MAST 4D3

Time off__________

Time on__________

Total time__________

CDX Tasksheet Number: C931

Vehicle used for this activity:

Year __________ Make ____________________ Model____________________

Odometer________________ VIN________________________________

1. **Research the function of the active suspension and stability control systems in the appropriate service information.**
   a. **Describe, in your own words, the function of the active suspension and stability control systems:**

2. **Have your supervisor/instructor verify satisfactory completion of your answers.**

Performance Rating

CDX Tasksheet Number: C931

0	1	2	3	4

Supervisor/instructor signature ______________________________ Date __________

▶ TASK Identify hybrid vehicle power steering system electrical circuits and safety precautions.

MAST 4B19

Time off________

Time on________

Total time________

CDX Tasksheet Number: C551

Vehicle used for this activity:

Year ________ Make ________ Model________

Odometer________ VIN________

1. **Research the location and safety precautions for the power steering system the vehicle is equipped with in the appropriate service information.**
   a. **List the voltage that the power steering system operates at: ________ V**
   b. **List any safety precautions when working on or around the power steering systems and circuits:**

2. **What color wires are used on the hybrid vehicle power steering system electrical circuits?**

3. **On the vehicle, locate and point out the power steering electrical circuits and components to your instructor.**

4. **Have your supervisor/instructor verify satisfactory completion of your answers.**

Performance Rating

CDX Tasksheet Number: C551

☐	☐	☐	☐	☐
0	1	2	3	4

Supervisor/instructor signature ________ Date ________

▶ TASK Inspect for power steering fluid leakage; determine needed action.

MAST 4B11

Time off________

Time on________

Total time________

CDX Tasksheet Number: C179

Vehicle used for this activity:

Year ____________ Make ________________________ Model________________________

Odometer____________________ VIN____

> NOTE If the vehicle's engine assembly is coated with leaking fluids and road dirt, you may need to pressure wash the engine compartment before inspecting for leaks. Get your instructor's permission before performing a cleaning operation.

> NOTE Some very small leaks, or leaks in engines that have a lot of accumulated residue, may be best diagnosed with the use of a fluorescent dye and ultraviolet light. Check with your instructor if this vehicle is a good candidate for that procedure. If so, follow the dye check equipment manufacturer's instructions for performing this test.

1. **Using a good light, inspect under the hood for any power steering fluid leaks. Inspect the reservoir, pump (including shaft seal), hoses, and fittings. List your observation(s):**

> NOTE Remember that gravity tends to pull any leaking fluid down. You may need to identify the highest point of the leak to locate the source.

2. **Safely raise and support the vehicle on the hoist.**
3. **Inspect the power steering pump, hoses, and gear box for leaks. Identify and list the source(s) of any leak(s):**
4. **Determine necessary action(s):**
5. **Have your supervisor/instructor verify satisfactory completion of this procedure, any observations found, and any necessary action(s) recommended.**

Performance Rating

CDX Tasksheet Number: C179

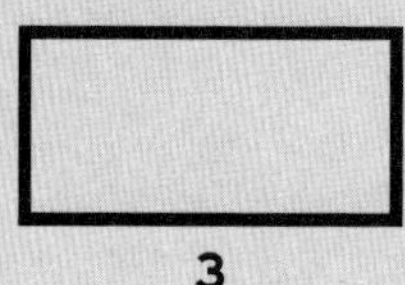

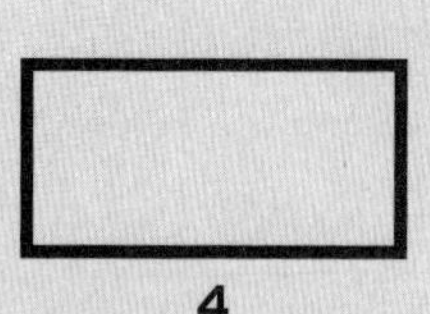

☐	☐	☐	☐	☐
0	1	2	3	4

Supervisor/instructor signature ________________________________ Date ____________

▶ TASK Diagnose power steering gear (non-rack and pinion) binding, uneven turning effort, looseness, hard steering, and noise concerns; determine needed action.

MAST 4B4

Time off________

Time on________

Total time________

CDX Tasksheet Number: C884

1. **List the power steering system-related customer concern:**

2. **Verify the concern and list your observations here:**

3. **Research the possible causes for this concern in the appropriate service information.**
    a. **List or print off and attach to this sheet the possible causes:**

    b. **List or print off and attach to this sheet the procedure for diagnosing the concern:**

4. **Follow the specified procedure to diagnose the concern. List your tests and results here:**

5. **List the cause of the concern:**

6. **Determine any necessary action(s) to correct the fault:**

7. **Have your supervisor/instructor verify satisfactory completion of this procedure, any observations found, and any necessary action(s) recommended.**

Performance Rating

CDX Tasksheet Number: C884

0	1	2	3	4
☐	☐	☐	☐	☐

Supervisor/instructor signature _______________ Date _______________

▶ TASK Diagnose power steering gear (rack and pinion) binding, uneven turning effort, looseness, hard steering, and noise concerns; determine needed action.

MAST 4B5

Time off________

Time on________

Total time________

CDX Tasksheet Number: C880

Vehicle used for this activity:

Year __________ Make __________________ Model__________________

Odometer______________ VIN____________________________

1. **List the power steering system-related customer concern:**

2. **Verify the concern and list your observations here:**

3. **Research the possible causes for this concern in the appropriate service information.**
   a. **List or print off and attach to this sheet the possible causes:**

   b. **List or print off and attach to this sheet the procedure for diagnosing the concern:**

4. **Follow the specified procedure to diagnose the concern. List your tests and results here:**

5. **List the cause of the concern:**

6. **Determine any necessary action(s) to correct the fault:**

7. **Have your supervisor/instructor verify satisfactory completion of this procedure, any observations found, and any necessary action(s) recommended.**

Performance Rating

CDX Tasksheet Number: C880

0	1	2	3	4
☐	☐	☐	☐	☐

Supervisor/instructor signature ______________________________ Date ______________

▶ TASK Diagnose steering column noises, looseness, and binding concerns (including tilt/telescoping mechanisms); determine needed action.

Time off________

Time on________

Total time________

CDX Tasksheet Number: C170

Vehicle used for this activity:

Year ______________ Make ____________________________ Model____________________________

Odometer_______________________ VIN____

1. **List the steering column-related customer concern:**

2. **Verify the concern and list your observations here:**

3. **Research the possible causes for this concern in the appropriate service information.**
    a. **List or print off and attach to this sheet the possible causes:**

    b. **List or print off and attach to this sheet the procedure for diagnosing the concern:**

    c. **List the precautions when working on this steering column:**

4. **Follow the specified procedure to diagnose the concern. List your tests and results here:**

5. **List the cause of the concern:**

6. **Determine any necessary action(s) to correct this fault:**

7. **Have your supervisor/instructor verify satisfactory completion of this procedure, any observations found, and any necessary action(s) recommended.**

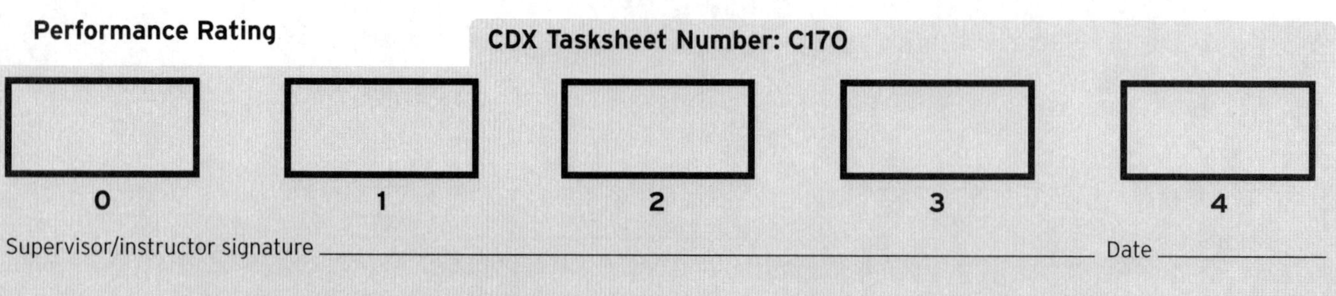

Performance Rating

CDX Tasksheet Number: C170

0	1	2	3	4

Supervisor/instructor signature ______________________ Date __________

▶ TASK Inspect proper power steering fluid level and condition. MAST 4B9

Time off________

Time on________

Total time________

CDX Tasksheet Number: C177

1. **Research specified power steering fluid for this vehicle using the appropriate service information.**
    a. **Specified fluid:** ____________________
    b. **When should the fluid be checked? Hot:** ________ **Cold:** ________ **Either:** ________
    c. **If the service information lists a procedure for flushing the power steering fluid, list the main steps (you can paraphrase, or print off the procedure):**

2. **Follow the manufacturer's procedure to check the fluid level.**

> NOTE If power steering fluid is below the minimum level, it could mean there is a leak in the system. Investigate this possibility and report it to your supervisor/instructor.

3. **Locate the power steering-fluid reservoir.**
    a. **List the level of the power steering fluid:** ________

4. **Place a small amount of the fluid from the reservoir on a white piece of paper and describe its condition:**

5. **Determine any necessary action(s):**

6. **Have your supervisor/instructor verify satisfactory completion of this procedure, any observations found, and any necessary action(s) recommended.**

Performance Rating

CDX Tasksheet Number: C177

☐	☐	☐	☐	☐
0	1	2	3	4

Supervisor/instructor signature ____________________ Date ________

▶ TASK Flush, fill, and bleed power steering system; use proper fluid type per manufacturer specification.

MAST 4B10

Time off________

Time on________

Total time________

CDX Tasksheet Number: C178

1. **Follow the specified procedure to flush the power steering fluid. If no procedure is specified, ask your supervisor/instructor to approve the following procedure:** ____________________
   a. **With the engine off, place a drain pan under the power steering pump return hose and out of the way of the fan or other moving parts.**
   b. **Remove the return hose from the power steering pump. Place the return hose in the drain pan. Plug the return line fitting in the power steering pump with an appropriate plug or cap.**
   c. **Determine the proper fluid per manufacturer specification. Fill the reservoir to the proper level with new fluid. Have an assistant start the engine and slowly turn the steering wheel to flush out the old fluid. At the same time, continue to add fluid to the reservoir (with the funnel) to keep it approximately full. Continue this until clean fluid comes out of the return line and then turn off the vehicle.**
   d. **Reinstall the return line and fill the reservoir to the proper level.**
   e. **Start the vehicle again and turn the steering wheel a few times from lock to lock. Check the fluid level and top off as necessary.**
   f. **If a buzzing noise is heard, there is probably air trapped in the system. In this case, turn off the engine, raise the front wheels off the ground (support the vehicle on jack stands or a hoist), and turn the wheels from lock to lock with the engine off. Do this several times. Check the fluid level and top off if necessary. Lower the vehicle. Restart the engine and listen and feel for proper operation. Repeat if necessary.**
   g. **Properly dispose of the old power steering fluid.**
   h. **List your observations:**

2. **Have your supervisor/instructor verify satisfactory completion of this procedure, any observations found, and any necessary action(s) recommended.**

Performance Rating

CDX Tasksheet Number: C178

☐	☐	☐	☐	☐
0	1	2	3	4

Supervisor/instructor signature ____________________ Date ________

▶ TASK Remove, inspect, replace, and/or adjust power steering pump drive belt.

MAST 4B12

Time off________

Time on________

Total time________

CDX Tasksheet Number: C180

1. **Using the service information, list the following:**
   a. **Type of power steering fluid:**

      ____

   b. **Type of belt: V-belt:** ________ **Serpentine belt:** ________
      Stretch Fit belt: ________ **Toothed belt:** ________
   c. **Belt-adjustment mechanism: N/A:** ________ **Manual:** ________
      Automatic: ________
   d. **Belt tension, if specified:** ______________________
   e. **Draw or print off and attach to this sheet the belt-routing diagram:**

2. **Following the recommended procedure, loosen the adjustment mechanism and remove the power steering pump drive belt. If equipped with a Stretch Fit belt it may be necessary to cut the old belt.**

3. **Examine the belt for cracks, splints, frayed surfaces, and distorted configurations (including stretching). Record your observation(s):**

4. **Examine the drive pulleys for any damage. Record your observation(s):**

5. **Have your supervisor/instructor verify removal. Supervisor's/instructor's initials:** ____________

> NOTE You may want to skip ahead and perform the next task C181: Remove and reinstall power steering pump while you have the belt removed. If so, return to this point when you are ready to reinstall the drive belt.

6. Following the specified procedure, replace the drive belt. If equipped with a Stretch Fit belt you will need a special installation tool, follow the manufacturer's instructions carefully.

7. Check the drive belt alignment in relation to the drive pulleys. List your observation(s):

8. Adjust the drive belt tension to the shop manufacturer's specifications (on the manually adjusted system).

   a. Measure the belt tension: ____________________

9. Check the fluid level in the power steering reservoir. Top off with the proper fluid, if necessary.

10. Start the engine and turn the steering wheel from lock to lock. Check for the following:

    a. Binding: Yes: ________ No: ________
    b. Excessive steering effort: Yes: ________ No: ________
    c. Uneven steering effort: Yes: ________ No: ________

11. Turn the engine off.

12. Re-measure the drive belt tension and list here: ____________________

13. Have your supervisor/instructor verify satisfactory completion of this procedure, any observations found, and any necessary action(s) recommended.

Performance Rating

CDX Tasksheet Number: C180

0	1	2	3	4

Supervisor/instructor signature ____________________ Date ____________

▶ TASK Remove and reinstall power steering pump.

MAST 4B13

Time off________

Time on________

Total time________

CDX Tasksheet Number: C181

1. **Research the procedure to remove and install the power steering pump. List the steps or print off the procedure:**

2. **Following the specified procedure, remove the power steering pump being careful not to damage any fittings or hoses. Also, pay close attention to the positioning of any brackets and spacers.**

3. **Inspect the pump and pulley. List your observation(s):**

4. **Have your supervisor/instructor verify removal. Supervisor's/instructor's initials: ________**

> NOTE You may want to skip ahead and perform the next task C699: Remove and reinstall press fit power steering pump pulley; check pulley and belt alignment while you have the pump removed. If so, return to this point when you are ready to reinstall the pump.

5. **Following the specified procedure, reinstall the power steering pump. Be careful to properly align all brackets, fittings, and hoses. Also, tighten all fasteners to their specified torque.**

6. **Have your supervisor/instructor verify satisfactory completion of this procedure, any observations found, and any necessary action(s) recommended.**

> NOTE Return to step 6 of task C180: Remove, inspect, replace, and/or adjust power steering pump drive belt to complete that task.

Performance Rating

CDX Tasksheet Number: C181

☐	☐	☐	☐	☐
0	1	2	3	4

Supervisor/instructor signature ________________ Date ________

▶ TASK Remove and reinstall press fit power steering pump pulley; check pulley and belt alignment.

MAST 4B14

Time off__________

Time on__________

Total time__________

CDX Tasksheet Number: C699

1. **Research the procedure to remove and install the power steering pump pulley in the appropriate service information. List the steps or print off the procedure:**

2. **Using the appropriate tools, remove the press fit power steering pump drive pulley from the drive shaft and inspect the pulley for any damage. List your observation(s):**

3. **Inspect the pump drive shaft and shaft seal for any damage. List your observation(s):**

4. **Have your supervisor/instructor verify removal. Supervisor's/instructor's initials:** __________

5. **Reinstall the press fit drive pulley on the power steering pump using the appropriate tool(s).**

> NOTE Return to task **C180: Remove, inspect, replace, and/or adjust power steering pump drive belt** step 6 to complete that task.

6. **Have your supervisor/instructor verify satisfactory completion of this procedure, any observations found, and any necessary action(s) recommended.**

Performance Rating

CDX Tasksheet Number: C699

☐	☐	☐	☐	☐
0	1	2	3	4

Supervisor/instructor signature ____________________ Date __________

▶ TASK Inspect, remove, and/or replace power steering hoses and fittings. MAST 4B15

Time off________

Time on________

Total time________

CDX Tasksheet Number: C183

1. **Research the procedure to remove and install the power steering hoses and fittings. List the steps or print off the procedure:**

2. **Following the specified procedure, drain the power steering fluid into a clean container for proper disposal according to environmental guidelines and regulations.**

3. **Disconnect power steering hoses from both the power steering pump and the power steering box or rack. Plug any exposed fittings to prevent entry of dirt or debris.**

4. **Disconnect any retaining clips.**

5. **Remove power steering hoses from the vehicle and place on your workbench.**

6. **Examine the flexible hoses for cracks, splits, chafed surfaces, and distorted configurations (including hardening and loss of flexibility). List your observation(s):**

7. **Examine any steel tubes and fittings, check for heat damage, splits, kinking, damaged threads, or restrictions. List your observation(s):**

8. **Have your supervisor/instructor verify removal. Supervisor's/instructor's initials: ________**

9. **Following the specified procedure, reinstall the power steering hoses being careful not to cross-thread any fittings or damage any hoses or tubes.**

10. **Have your supervisor/instructor verify satisfactory completion of this procedure, any observations found, and any necessary action(s) recommended.**

Performance Rating

CDX Tasksheet Number: C183

0	1	2	3	4
☐	☐	☐	☐	☐

Supervisor/instructor signature ________________________ Date ________

▶ TASK Test power steering system pressure; determine needed action.

MAST 4B20

Time off________

Time on________

Total time________

CDX Tasksheet Number: C1001

1. **Research the procedure to pressure test the power steering system. List the steps or print off the procedure:**

2. **Following the recommended procedure, prepare the vehicle to perform the power steering system pressure test.**

3. **Connect the pressure tester to the vehicle.**

4. **With the pressure gauge control valve open, start the engine and run at idle until the air is purged from the system. Turn the engine off. Check the fluid level and check for leaks.**

5. **Start the engine and record the initial pressure ____________ and flow ____________ readings on the gauge. Close and open the pressure gauge control valve two or three times. (Never hold the valve closed more than five seconds.) Record the highest pressure indicated on the gauge. ____________ psi/kPa**

6. **With the control valve open, turn the steering wheel to the extreme left and to the extreme right. Record the highest indicated pressure. ____________ psi/kPa**

7. **Compare these readings to the specifications, and take the results to your supervisor.**

8. **Remove the analyzer from the vehicle. (CAUTION: The fluid may be extremely hot.) Reconnect the hoses using new O-rings.**

9. **Top off the power steering reservoir and follow the manufacturer's procedure to bleed any air from the system.**

10. **Check the power steering system for any leaks.**

11. **Determine any needed action.**

12. **Have your supervisor/instructor verify satisfactory completion of this proce→dure, any observations found, and any necessary action(s) recommended.**

Performance Rating

CDX Tasksheet Number: C1001

☐	☐	☐	☐	☐
0	1	2	3	4

Supervisor/instructor signature ______________________________ Date ____________

▶ TASK Remove and replace rack and pinion steering gear; inspect mounting bushings and brackets.

MAST 4B7

Time off__________

Time on__________

Total time__________

CDX Tasksheet Number: C882

1. **Research the following procedures and specifications in the appropriate service information.**
   a. **R & R rack and pinion flat rate time: ________________ hrs**
   b. **R & R inner tie rod end (either side) flat rate time: ________________ hrs**
   c. **Type of power steering fluid:**
   ____
   d. **Rack and pinion steering gear removal. List the main steps (you can paraphrase or print off the procedure):**

2. **Start the engine and straighten the wheels. Turn the engine off and lock the steering column. This will keep the clock spring centered.**

3. **Follow the service information procedure to remove the rack and pinion steering gear. Be careful not to damage any lines, tubes, or fittings. Plug any lines or fittings to prevent entry of dirt or debris.**

4. **Inspect the condition of the mounting bushings and brackets. List your observations:**

   a. **Have your supervisor/instructor verify removal. Supervisor's/instructor's initials ________________**

> NOTE You may want to skip to task **C883: Inspect rack and pinion steering gear inner tie rod ends (sockets) and bellows boots; replace as needed**. This task will be much easier to perform with the rack and pinion removed from the vehicle. If so, return to this point when you are ready to reinstall the rack and pinion.

5. **Follow the service information procedure to reinstall the rack and pinion steering gear. Be careful not to damage any lines, tubes, or fittings. Also, unless the manufacturer directs otherwise, make sure the rack is centered in its travel so that the clock spring will be indexed to the rack.**

6. **Torque all fasteners and fittings.**

7. **Check the fluid level in the power steering reservoir. Top off with the proper fluid.**

8. **Start the engine and bleed any air from the power steering system. Top off fluid as necessary.**

9. With the engine running, turn the steering wheel from lock to lock. Check for the following:
    a. Binding: Yes: ____________ No: ____________
    b. Excessive steering effort: Yes: ____________ No: ____________
    c. Uneven steering effort: Yes: ____________ No: ____________

10. Have your supervisor/instructor verify satisfactory completion of this procedure, any observations found, and any necessary action(s) recommended.

Performance Rating

CDX Tasksheet Number: C882

☐	☐	☐	☐	☐
0	1	2	3	4

Supervisor/instructor signature ______________________________ Date ____________

▶ TASK Inspect rack and pinion steering gear inner tie rod ends (sockets) and bellows boots; replace as needed.

MAST 4B8

Time off__________

Time on__________

Total time__________

CDX Tasksheet Number: C883

1. **Following the service information procedure, inspect the tie rod ends (sockets) and bellows boots. List your observation(s):**

2. **Determine which inner tie rod end your supervisor/instructor would like you to remove:**

3. **Remove the bellows boot to gain access to the inner tie rod.**

4. **Following the service information procedure, extend the rack (by turning the pinion shaft) to expose the locking nut of the inner tie rod socket. Using the appropriate tools, loosen the inner tie rod socket and unscrew the tie rod end.**

5. **Inspect the components and list your observations:**

6. **Have your supervisor/instructor verify removal. Supervisor's/instructor's initials: ____________________**

7. **Following the service information procedure, reassemble the inner tie rod socket and torque to the manufacturer's specifications.**

8. **Have your supervisor/instructor verify proper torque. Supervisor's/instructor's initials: ____________________**

9. **Reassemble the bellows boot and secure it according to the manufacturer's procedure.**

10. **Have your supervisor/instructor verify satisfactory completion of this procedure, any observations found, and any necessary action(s) recommended.**

Performance Rating

CDX Tasksheet Number: C883

☐	☐	☐	☐	☐
0	1	2	3	4

Supervisor/instructor signature ______________________________ Date __________

▶ TASK Inspect, remove, and/or replace pitman arm, relay (centerlink/intermediate) rod, idler arm, mountings, and steering linkage damper.

MAST 4B16

Time off________

Time on________

Total time________

CDX Tasksheet Number: C184

1. **Research the following specifications and procedures in the appropriate service information.**
   a. **Maximum allowable play in each of the steering linkage joints:**

2. **Lift and support the vehicle according to the procedure listed in the service information.**

3. **Follow the manufacturer's procedure and inspect the steering system parts listed. List your observation(s):**
   a. **Pitman arm:**

   b. **Relay (centerlink/intermediate) rod:**

   c. **Idler arm and mountings:**

   d. **Steering linkage damper, if equipped:**

   e. **Tie rod ends:**

f. **Tie rod sleeves and clamps:**

4. **Following the manufacturer's procedure, mark the location of the pitman arm shaft and pitman arm splines. Disconnect the pitman arm from the relay (centerlink/intermediate) rod steering linkage.**

5. **Remove the pitman arm-retaining nut and, using the manufacturer's recommended removal tool, remove the pitman arm.**

6. **If the vehicle is fitted with a steering damper, remove the steering damper and place it on your workbench.**

7. **Disconnect the relay (centerlink/intermediate) rod steering linkage.**

8. **Remove idler arm assembly.**

9. **Remove tie rod ends from steering knuckles.**

NOTE The use of a pickle fork will damage the dust boots. Only use this tool on joints you will be replacing. On joints you will be reusing, try the hammer method to break the joint free. See your instructor for details.

10. **Loosen the tie rod adjusting sleeve clamp bolts. Remove tie rod ends from sleeves.**

NOTE Count the number of turns as you back out each tie rod from its sleeve so you can reinstall it in approximately the same position. This will assist in making the wheel alignment easier to perform.

11. **Inspect all components and list your observations:**

12. **Have your supervisor/instructor verify removal. Supervisor's/instructor's initials: ___________**

13. **Reassemble all components following the manufacturer's recommended procedure, being sure to torque all fasteners and secure all joints with new cotter pins (or other approved method).**

    a. **List the torque you tightened the tie rod nuts to: _____________ ft-lb/N·m**
    b. **List the torque you tightened the tie rod adjusting sleeve nuts to: _____________ ft-lb/N·m**
    c. **Did you replace all removed cotter pins with new cotter pins? Yes: _________ No: _________**

14 **Start the vehicle and check for binding or improper steering operation. List your observations:**

> **NOTE** Before this vehicle can be driven, it MUST have a wheel alignment performed. Failure to do so means this is an unsafe vehicle, which could result in substantial injury or even death.

15. **Have your supervisor/instructor verify satisfactory completion of this procedure, any observations found, and any necessary action(s) recommended.**

Performance Rating

CDX Tasksheet Number: C184

☐	☐	☐	☐	☐
0	1	2	3	4

Supervisor/instructor signature ______________________ Date __________

▶ TASK Inspect, replace, and/or adjust tie rod ends (sockets), tie rod sleeves, and clamps.

MAST 4B17

Time off________

Time on________

Total time________

CDX Tasksheet Number: C185

1. **Research the following specifications and procedures in the appropriate service information.**
    a. **Maximum allowable play in the tie rod ends:**

2. **Lift and support the vehicle according to the procedure listed in the service information.**

3. **Follow the manufacturer's procedure and inspect the steering system parts listed. List your observation(s):**
    a. **Tie rod ends:**

    b. **Tie rod sleeves and clamps:**

4. **Determine any necessary actions:**

5. **Remove tie rod ends from steering knuckles.**

> **NOTE** The use of a pickle fork will damage the dust boots. Only use this tool on joints you will be replacing. On joints you will be reusing, try the hammer method to break the joint free. See your instructor for details.

6. **Loosen the tie rod adjusting sleeve clamp bolts. Remove tie rod ends from sleeves.**

> **NOTE** Count the number of turns as you back out each tie rod from its sleeve so you can reinstall it in approximately the same position. This will assist in making the wheel alignment easier to perform.

7. **Inspect all components and list your observations:**

8. **Have your supervisor/instructor verify removal. Supervisor's/instructor's initials: ________**

9. **Reassemble all components following the manufacturer's specified procedure, being sure to torque all fasteners and secure all joints with new cotter pins (or other approved method).**
    a. **List the torque you tightened the tie rod nuts to: __________ ft-lb/N·m**
    b. **List the torque you tightened the tie rod adjusting sleeve nuts to: __________ ft-lb/N·m**
    c. **Did you replace all removed cotter pins with new cotter pins? Yes: ________ No: ________**

10. **Start the vehicle and check for binding or improper steering operation. List your observations:**

> NOTE Before this vehicle can be driven, it MUST have a wheel alignment performed. Failure to do so means this is an unsafe vehicle which could result in substantial injury or even death.

11. **Have your supervisor/instructor verify satisfactory completion of this procedure, any observations found, and any necessary action(s) recommended.**

Performance Rating

CDX Tasksheet Number: C185

☐	☐	☐	☐	☐
0	1	2	3	4

Supervisor/instructor signature ______________________ Date ________

▶ TASK Inspect, test, and diagnose electrically assisted power steering systems (including using a scan tool); determine needed action.

MAST 4B18

Time off________

Time on________

Total time________

CDX Tasksheet Number: C186

Vehicle used for this activity:

Year ______________ Make ____________________________ Model ______________________________

Odometer______________________ VIN____

1. **List the electronically controlled steering system-related customer concern:**

2. **Verify the concern and list your observations:**

3. **Retrieve any DTCs with a scan tool and list those DTCs:**

4. **Research the possible causes for this concern in the appropriate service information.**
    a. **List or print off and attach to this sheet the possible causes:**

    b. **List or print off and attach to this sheet the procedure for diagnosing the concern:**

5. **Follow the specified procedure to diagnose the concern. List your tests and results:**

6. **List the cause of the concern:**

7. **Determine any necessary action(s) to correct the fault:**

8. **Have your supervisor/instructor verify satisfactory completion of this procedure, any observations found, and any necessary action(s) recommended.**

Performance Rating

CDX Tasksheet Number: C186

0	1	2	3	4
☐	☐	☐	☐	☐

Supervisor/instructor signature ________________ Date ________

▶ TASK Demonstrate awareness of the safety aspects of supplemental restraint systems (SRS), electronic brake control systems, and hybrid vehicle high voltage circuits.

MAST
OA13

Time off________

Time on________

Total time________

CDX Tasksheet Number: C464

1. **Research the following procedures for a hybrid vehicle in the appropriate service information.**
    a. **List the precautions when working around or on the SRS system on this vehicle:**

    b. **List the steps to disable the SRS system on this vehicle:**

    c. **List the steps to enable the SRS system on this vehicle:**

    d. **List the precautions when working on or around the electronic brake control system on this vehicle:**

e. **Identify the high-voltage circuit wiring on this vehicle. What color is the wire conduit?**

f. **List or print out the high-voltage disable procedure for this vehicle.**

2. **Have your supervisor/instructor verify satisfactory completion of this task.**

Performance Rating

CDX Tasksheet Number: C464

0	1	2	3	4

Supervisor/instructor signature ______________________ Date ________

▶ TASK Disable and enable supplemental restraint system (SRS); verify indicator lamp operation.

MAST 4B1

Time off________

Time on________

Total time________

CDX Tasksheet Number: C168

1. **Locate "disable vehicle SRS system" in the appropriate service information for the vehicle you are working on.**
    a. **List or print off and attach to this sheet the safety precautions to be taken when disabling the SRS system:**

    b. **List or print off and attach to this sheet the steps to disable the SRS system:**

    c. **List or print off and attach to this sheet the steps to enable the SRS system:**

2. **Have your supervisor/instructor verify your listed procedures. Supervisor's/instructor's initials:** ________________
3. **Disarm the SRS system.**
4. **Have your supervisor/instructor verify that the SRS is disabled. Supervisor's/instructor's initials:** ________________

> NOTE You may want to consider skipping to task C169: Remove and replace steering wheel; center/time supplemental restraint system (SRS) coil (clock spring) since it requires disabling the SRS. Return to this step when you complete that task and re-enable the SRS.

5. **Following the specified procedure, enable the vehicle's SRS.**
6. **Following the specified procedure, verify indicator lamp operation.**

7. **Have your supervisor/instructor verify satisfactory completion of this procedure, any observations found, and any necessary action(s) recommended.**

Performance Rating

CDX Tasksheet Number: 168

0	1	2	3	4
☐	☐	☐	☐	☐

Supervisor/instructor signature _______________ Date _______

▶ TASK Remove and replace steering wheel; center/time supplemental restraint system (SRS) coil (clock spring).

MAST 4B2

Time off________

Time on________

Total time________

CDX Tasksheet Number: C169

1. **Locate "remove and replace steering wheel" and "center/time SRS clock spring" procedures in the appropriate service information.**
   a. **List or print off and attach to this sheet the procedures for removing and replacing the steering wheel:**

   b. **List or print off and attach to this sheet the procedure to center/time the SRS clock spring:**

2. **Have your supervisor/instructor verify your listed procedures. Supervisor's/instructor's initials: ________________**
3. **Following the specified procedures and precautions, remove the steering wheel.**
4. **Following the specified procedures and precautions, remove the clock spring.**
5. **Inspect the components and list your observation(s):**

6. **Have your supervisor/instructor verify the removal of these components. Supervisor's/instructor's initials: ________________**
7. **Reassemble the steering column. Be sure to follow all manufacturer-recommended procedures and precautions.**

> **NOTE** Return to task step 5 of C168: Disable and enable supplemental restraint system (SRS); verify indicator lamp operation to enable the SRS.

8. **Have your supervisor/instructor verify satisfactory completion of this procedure, any observations found, and any necessary action(s) recommended.**

Performance Rating

CDX Tasksheet Number: C169

☐	☐	☐	☐	☐
0	1	2	3	4

Supervisor/instructor signature ________________________________ Date ____________

▶ TASK Inspect steering shaft universal joint(s), flexible coupling(s), collapsible column, lock cylinder mechanism, and steering wheel; determine needed action.

Time off__________

Time on__________

Total time__________

CDX Tasksheet Number: C173

1. **If the vehicle is fitted with an SRS, disable it according to the manufacturer's procedure and precautions.**
2. **Safely raise and support the vehicle so the tires are a few inches off the floor.**
3. **With the steering column lock activated, try to turn the steering wheel from side to side.**
   a. **Is the locking mechanism working? Yes: __________ No: __________**
   b. **List your observation(s):**
4. **With the engine ignition key in the "off" position, ensure the steering lock is not engaged and have an assistant rock the steering wheel from side to side (just enough to move the road wheels slightly). While the steering wheel is being rocked, check for any wear or looseness in the shaft universal joint(s) or flexible coupling(s).**
   a. **List your observation(s):**
5. **Following the specified procedure, check that the steering column collapsible action has not been compromised.**
   a. **List your observation(s):**
6. **Check the steering wheel for the following and list any observation(s):**
   a. **Looseness on the steering shaft:**
   b. **Structural damage:**

c. **SRS airbag is intact and has appropriate pad/cover:**

d. **Size and appropriateness for the make and model of the vehicle (refer to the service information):**

7. **Have your supervisor/instructor verify your observations. Supervisor's/instructor's initials: ____________________**

8. **Perform any necessary action(s) and list them here:**

9. **Following the specified procedure, enable the SRS.**

10. **Have your supervisor/instructor verify satisfactory completion of this procedure, any observations found, and any necessary action(s) recommended.**

Performance Rating

CDX Tasksheet Number: C173

☐	☐	☐	☐	☐
0	1	2	3	4

Supervisor/instructor signature ______________________________ Date ____________

▶ TASK Diagnose short and long arm suspension system noises, body sway, and uneven ride height concerns; determine needed action.

MAST 4C1

Time off________

Time on________

Total time________

CDX Tasksheet Number: C852

1. **List the short and long arm suspension system-related customer concern:**

2. **Verify the concern and list your observations here:**

3. **Research the possible causes for this concern in the appropriate service information:**
   a. **List or print off and attach to this sheet the possible causes:**
   b. **List or print off and attach to this sheet the procedure for diagnosing the concern:**

4. **Follow the service-specified procedure to diagnose the concern. List your tests and results here:**

5. **List the cause of the concern:**

6. **Determine any necessary action(s) to correct the fault:**

7. **Have your supervisor/instructor verify satisfactory completion of this procedure, any observations found, and any necessary action(s) recommended.**

Performance Rating

CDX Tasksheet Number: C852

☐	☐	☐	☐	☐
0	1	2	3	4

Supervisor/instructor signature _______________ Date _______

▶ TASK Diagnose strut suspension system noises, body sway, and uneven ride height concerns; determine needed action.

MAST
4C2

Time off________

Time on________

Total time________

CDX Tasksheet Number: C853

Vehicle used for this activity:

Year ________ Make ________________ Model________________

Odometer____________ VIN________________________

1. **List the strut suspension system-related customer concern:**

2. **Verify the concern and list your observations here:**

3. **Research the possible causes for this concern in the appropriate service information.**
   a. **List or print off and attach to this sheet the possible causes:**

   b. **List or print off and attach to this sheet the procedure for diagnosing the concern:**

4. **Follow the specified procedure to diagnose the concern. List your tests and results here:**

5. **List the cause of the concern:**

6. **Determine any necessary action(s) to correct the fault:**

7. **Have your supervisor/instructor verify satisfactory completion of this procedure, any observations found, and any necessary action(s) recommended.**

Performance Rating

CDX Tasksheet Number: C853

0	1	2	3	4
☐	☐	☐	☐	☐

Supervisor/instructor signature _______________ Date _______

▶ TASK Diagnose vehicle wander, drift, pull, hard steering, bump steer, memory steer, torque steer, and steering return concerns; determine needed action.

MAST 4E1

Time off______

Time on______

Total time______

CDX Tasksheet Number: C206

1. **List the wheel alignment-related customer concern:**

2. **Verify the concern and list your observations here:**

3. **Research the possible causes for this concern in the appropriate service information.**
    a. **List or print off and attach to this sheet the possible causes:**

    b. **List or print off and attach to this sheet the procedure for diagnosing the concern:**

4. **Reflecting back over these tasks, complete the three Cs, which you stated previously.**
    a. **List the customer concern(s):**

b. List the cause(s) of the concern(s):

c. List the action(s) necessary to correct the fault(s):

5. Have your supervisor/instructor verify satisfactory completion of this procedure, any observations found, and any necessary action(s) recommended.

Performance Rating

CDX Tasksheet Number: C206

☐	☐	☐	☐	☐
0	1	2	3	4

Supervisor/instructor signature ______________________ Date ________

▶ TASK Inspect, remove, and/or replace front/rear stabilizer bar (sway bar) bushings, brackets, and links.

Time off________

Time on________

Total time________

CDX Tasksheet Number: C793

1. **Research the disassembly and inspection procedure for the stabilizer bar, bushings, brackets, and links in the appropriate service information.**
    a. **List any precautions:**

    b. **List or print off and attach to this sheet the steps to disassemble the stabilizer bar system.**

2. **Safely raise and support the vehicle.**

3. **Following the specified procedure outlined in the service information, inspect, dismantle, clean, and re-inspect the stabilizer bar, bushings, and links. List your observation(s):**
    a. **Stabilizer bar:**

    b. **Bushing(s):**

    c. **Link(s):**

4. **Determine any necessary action(s):**

5. **Have your supervisor/instructor verify satisfactory completion of this procedure, any observations found, and any necessary action(s) recommended.**

Performance Rating

CDX Tasksheet Number: C793

☐	☐	☐	☐	☐
0	1	2	3	4

Supervisor/instructor signature ______________________ Date ____________

▶ TASK Inspect, remove, and/or replace shock absorbers; inspect mounts and bushings.

MAST 4D1

Time off________

Time on________

Total time________

CDX Tasksheet Number: C202

1. **Research the shock absorber removal and installation procedure in the appropriate service information. Follow all directions.**
   a. **Shock absorber fastener torque: ________ ft-lb/N·m**
   b. **List the flat rate time for this job: ________ hrs**
2. **Carefully bounce check the shock absorbers by pushing on each corner of the bumpers. Let go at the bottom of the travel and observe how many oscillations it takes for the vehicle to come to a stop. List your observations:**
3. **Safely raise and support the vehicle on a hoist. Check to see that the vehicle is secure on the hoist, and then remove the shock absorbers following the service information procedures.**

> NOTE Be sure to support the suspension, or axle assembly, with safety stands before removing the shocks.

4. **Inspect the shock absorbers, rubber bushings (bushes), and mounts and list your observations:**
   a. **Shock absorbers:**
   b. **Rubber bushings (bushes):**
   c. **Shock mounts:**

5. **Determine any necessary action(s):**

6. **Have your supervisor/instructor verify the removal and your observations. Supervisor's/instructor's initials: ______________________**

7. **Reinstall the shock absorbers according to the specified procedure. Be sure to torque all fasteners properly.**

8. **Have your supervisor/instructor verify satisfactory completion of this procedure, any observations found, and any necessary action(s) recommended.**

Performance Rating

CDX Tasksheet Number: C202

☐	☐	☐	☐	☐
0	1	2	3	4

Supervisor/instructor signature ____ Date ____________

▶ TASK Inspect, remove, and/or replace short and long arm suspension system coil springs and spring insulators.

MAST 4C7

Time off________

Time on________

Total time________

CDX Tasksheet Number: C193

1. **Research the removal and inspection procedure for the coil springs and spring insulators in the appropriate service information.**
   a. **List any precautions:**

   b. **List or print off and attach to this sheet the steps to remove the coil springs.**

2. **Have your supervisor/instructor verify your listed precautions and procedures. Supervisor's/instructor's initials: ________**

3. **Following the specified procedure outlined in the service information, inspect, remove, clean, and re-inspect the coil spring and spring insulators. List your observation(s):**
   a. **Coil spring:**

   b. **Spring insulators:**

4. **Determine any necessary action(s):**

5. **Have your supervisor/instructor verify satisfactory completion of this procedure, any observations found, and any necessary action(s) recommended.**

Performance Rating

CDX Tasksheet Number: C193

☐	☐	☐	☐	☐
0	1	2	3	4

Supervisor/instructor signature _______________ Date _______________

▶ TASK Inspect, remove, and/or replace steering knuckle assemblies.

MAST
4C6

Time off________

Time on________

Total time________

CDX Tasksheet Number: C192

1. **Research the removal and inspection procedure for the steering knuckle assembly in the appropriate service information.**
   a. **List any precautions:**

   b. **List or print off and attach to this sheet the steps to remove the steering knuckle assembly.**

2. **Following the specified procedure outlined in the service information, inspect, remove, clean, and re-inspect the steering knuckle assembly. List your observation(s):**
   a. **Steering knuckle:**

3. **Determine any necessary action(s):**

4. **Have your supervisor/instructor verify satisfactory completion of this procedure, any observations found, and any necessary action(s) recommended.**

Performance Rating

CDX Tasksheet Number: C192

0	1	2	3	4
☐	☐	☐	☐	☐

Supervisor/instructor signature ______________________ Date ________

▶ TASK Inspect, remove, and/or replace upper and lower control arms, bushings, shafts, and rebound bumpers.

MAST 4C3

Time off________

Time on________

Total time________

CDX Tasksheet Number: C790

1. **Research the removal and inspection procedure for the upper and lower control arms, bushings, shafts, and rebound bumpers in the appropriate service information.**
   a. **List any precautions:**

   b. **List or print off and attach to this sheet the steps to remove the control arms.**

2. **Following the specified procedure outlined in the service information, inspect, remove, clean, and re-inspect the upper and lower control arms, bushings, shafts, and rebound bumpers. List your observation(s):**
   a. **Upper control arm:**

   b. **Lower control arm:**

   c. **Bushings:**

   d. **Shafts:**

   e. **Rebound bumper(s):**

3. **Determine any necessary action(s):**

4. **Have your supervisor/instructor verify satisfactory completion of this procedure, any observations found, and any necessary action(s) recommended.**

Performance Rating

CDX Tasksheet Number: C790

0	1	2	3	4
☐	☐	☐	☐	☐

Supervisor/instructor signature ______________________ Date ________

▶ TASK Inspect, remove, and/or replace strut rods and bushings.

MAST 4C4

Time off________

Time on________

Total time________

CDX Tasksheet Number: C791

1. **Research the inspection and disassembly procedure for the strut rods and bushings in the appropriate service information.**
   a. **List any precautions:**

   b. **List or print off and attach to this sheet the steps to inspect and disassemble the strut rods and bushings:**

2. **Following the specified procedure outlined in the service information, remove the strut rods and bushings from the vehicle. List your observation(s):**
   a. **Strut rod:**

   b. **Bushings:**

3. **Determine any necessary action(s):**

4. **Have your supervisor/instructor verify satisfactory completion of this procedure, any observations found, and any necessary action(s) recommended.**

Performance Rating

CDX Tasksheet Number: C791

0	1	2	3	4
☐	☐	☐	☐	☐

Supervisor/instructor signature ________________________ Date ________

▶ TASK Inspect, remove, and/or replace upper and/or lower ball joints (with or without wear indicators).

MAST 4C5

Time off________

Time on________

Total time________

CDX Tasksheet Number: C792

1. **Research the inspection and disassembly procedure for the upper and/or lower ball joints in the appropriate service information.**
   a. **Maximum allowable play in the lower ball joint: __________________ in/mm**
   b. **Maximum allowable play in the upper ball joint; if applicable: __________________ in/mm**
   c. **Which ball joint is the load-bearing ball joint? Lower: __________________ Upper: __________________**
   d. **List any precautions:**
   e. **List or print off and attach to this sheet the steps to inspect the lower and/or upper ball joints.**
   f. **List or print off and attach to this sheet the steps to disassemble the lower and/or upper ball joints.**
2. **Following the specified procedure, measure the play in the lower and/or upper ball joint(s). List your observation(s):**
   a. **Measure the play in the lower ball joint: Left ________ in/mm Right: ________ in/mm**
   b. **Measure the play in the upper ball joints: Left: ________ in/mm Right: ________ in/mm.**
3. **Following the specified procedure, remove, clean, and re-inspect the lower and/or upper ball joints. List your observation(s):**
4. **Determine any necessary action(s):**

5. **Have your instructor verify the removal of all suspension components and check your observations and necessary actions. Get permission to reassemble the assembly. Supervisor's/instructor's initials: ______________________**

> **NOTE** At this time, replace/reinstall all removed suspension components following the manufacturer's procedures and precautions. Be sure to tighten all fasteners to their specified torque and replace any retaining devices such as cotter pins (with new ones) and nylon locking nuts. Be careful to route all wires, hoses, and tubes in their original factory position.

6. **Inspect the reassembled suspension unit for any loose fasteners, improperly installed components, etc. List your observations here:**

7. **Determine any necessary action(s):**

8. **Have your supervisor/instructor verify satisfactory completion of this procedure, any observations found, and any necessary action(s) recommended.**

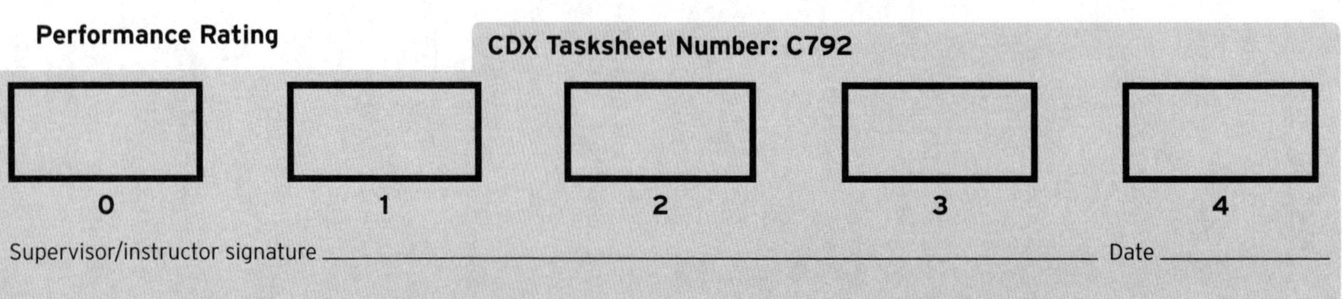

Performance Rating
CDX Tasksheet Number: C792
0
1
2
3
4
Supervisor/instructor signature
Date

▶ TASK Inspect, remove, and/or replace strut cartridge or assembly, strut coil spring, insulators (silencers), and upper-strut bearing mount.

MAST 4C10

Time off________

Time on________

Total time________

CDX Tasksheet Number: C794

1. **Research the disassembly and inspection procedure for the strut cartridge or assembly, strut coil spring, insulators (silencers), and upper-strut bearing mount in the appropriate service information.**
    a. **List any precautions:**

    b. **List or print off and attach to this sheet the steps to inspect, remove, and disassemble the strut assembly:**

2. **Have your supervisor/instructor verify your listed precautions and procedures. Supervisor's/instructor's initials: ________________**
3. **Safely raise and support the vehicle.**
4. **Following the specified procedure outlined in the service information, inspect the struts on the vehicle. List your observations:**

5. **Following the specified procedure, remove the strut assembly from the vehicle.**

> NOTE On some vehicles, it makes sense to mark the position of the adjustable components so they can be reinstalled into their original positions.

6. **Following the specified procedure outlined in the service information, disassemble the strut. Improperly removing the spring can cause severe injury or death.**
7. **Clean and inspect the strut cartridge or assembly, strut coil spring, insulators (silencers), and upper-strut bearing mount. List your observation(s):**
    a. **Strut cartridge or assembly:**

    b. **Strut coil spring:**

c. **Spring insulators:**

d. **Upper-strut bearing mount:**

8. **Determine any necessary action(s):**

9. **Have your instructor verify the removal and disassembly of the strut, and check your observations and necessary actions. Get permission to reassemble the strut. Supervisor's/instructor's initials: ________________**

10. **Reassemble the strut according to the manufacturer's procedure and precautions. Be careful when compressing and installing the spring as it can cause severe injury or death if installed improperly.**

11. **Reinstall the strut into the vehicle. Be sure to tighten all fasteners to their specified torque and replace any retaining devices such as cotter pins and nylon locking nuts. Be careful to route all wires, hoses, and tubes in their original factory positions.**

12. **Inspect the reassembled strut assembly for any loose fasteners, improperly installed components, etc. List your observations here:**

13. **Have your supervisor/instructor verify satisfactory completion of this procedure, any observations found, and any necessary action(s) recommended.**

Performance Rating

CDX Tasksheet Number: C794

☐	☐	☐	☐	☐
0	1	2	3	4

Supervisor/instructor signature ________________________________ Date __________

▶ TASK Inspect rear suspension system leaf spring(s), spring insulators (silencers), shackles, brackets, bushings, center pins/bolts, and mounts.

MAST 4C12

Time off________

Time on________

Total time________

CDX Tasksheet Number: C854

Vehicle used for this activity:

Year ________ Make ________ Model ________

Odometer ________ VIN ________

1. **Research the leaf-spring inspection procedure in the appropriate service information. Follow all directions.**
   a. **U-bolt torque: ________ ft-lb/N·m**
   b. **Shackle bolt torque: ________ ft-lb/N·m**

2. **Safely raise and support the vehicle. Support the axle assembly with safety stands.**

3. **Following the specified procedure, inspect and record the condition of each of the following:**
   a. **Rear-shackle bushings:**

   b. **Front-shackle bushings:**

   c. **Spring-leaf insulators:**

   d. **U-bolts and nuts:**

   e. **Rubber-bump stops:**

f. **Spring shackles and plates:**

g. **Leaf-spring pack:**

4. **Determine any necessary action(s):**

5. **Have your supervisor/instructor verify satisfactory completion of this procedure, any observations found, and any necessary action(s) recommended.**

Performance Rating

CDX Tasksheet Number: C854

0	1	2	3	4

Supervisor/instructor signature ____________________ Date ________

▶ TASK Remove, inspect, service, and/or replace front and rear wheel bearings.

MAST 4D2

Time off________

Time on________

Total time________

CDX Tasksheet Number: C203

Vehicle used for this activity:

Year ____________ Make ________________________ Model________________________

Odometer____________________ VIN____

1. **Which wheel bearing are you servicing?** ________________________

2. **What type of bearing is this vehicle equipped with? Serviceable:** __________ **Sealed:** __________

3. **Research the wheel-bearing removal, service, and installation procedure in the appropriate service information. Follow all directions.**
    a. **List the bearing adjustment procedure, if applicable:**

    b. **Specified wheel-bearing grease:** ________________________
    c. **Lug nut torque:** ________________________ **ft-lb/N·m**
    d. **List the flat rate time for this job:** ________________________ **hrs**

4. **Safely raise and support the vehicle.**

5. **Following the specified procedure, dismantle, clean, and inspect wheel bearing and race. List your observation(s):**
    a. **Wheel bearing:**

    b. **Race:**

    c. **Spindle:**

d. Hub:

e. Grease seal:

f. Are these parts serviceable? Yes: ________ No: ________

6. Determine any necessary action(s):

7. Have your supervisor/instructor verify the removal and your observations. Supervisor's/instructor's initials: ________________________

8. Repack (if applicable) the wheel bearings with the specified grease.

9. Following the specified procedure, reinstall and adjust the wheel-bearing assembly. Before locking the adjustment nut, have your supervisor/instructor verify the wheel-bearing adjustment. Supervisor's/instructor's initials: ________________________

10. Following the specified procedure, lock the wheel-bearing adjustment nut with the specified retaining device. Always replace disposable devices such as cotter pins with new parts.

11. Return the vehicle to its beginning condition and clean and return any tools that you may have used to their proper locations.

12. Have your supervisor/instructor verify satisfactory completion of this procedure, any observations found, and any necessary action(s) recommended.

Performance Rating

CDX Tasksheet Number: C203

☐	☐	☐	☐	☐
0	1	2	3	4

Supervisor/instructor signature ________________________ Date ____________

▶ TASK Inspect, remove, and/or replace track bar, strut rods/radius arms, and related mounts and bushings.

MAST 4C11

Time off________

Time on________

Total time________

CDX Tasksheet Number: C934

1. **Research the inspection and disassembly procedure for the track bars, strut rods/radius arms, mounts, and bushings in the appropriate service information.**
   a. **List or print off and attach to this sheet the steps to inspect and disassemble the track bars, strut rods/radius arms, mounts, and bushings:**

2. **Following the specified procedure outlined in the service information, remove the track bars, strut rods/radius arms, mounts, and bushings from the vehicle. List your observation(s):**
   a. **Track bars:**

   b. **Strut rod/radius arms:**

   c. **Mounts:**

   d. **Bushings:**

3. **Determine any necessary action(s):**

4. **Have your instructor verify the removal and disassembly of the track bars, strut rod/radius arms, mounts, and bushings, and check your observations and necessary actions. Also, have your instructor sign off on the disassembly of the strut in the previous task. Supervisor's/instructor's initials: ____________________**

5. **Reassemble the strut rods, mounts, and bushings according to the manufacturer's procedure and precautions.**

6. **Have your supervisor/instructor verify satisfactory completion of this procedure, any observations found, and any necessary action(s) recommended.**

Performance Rating

CDX Tasksheet Number: C934

0	1	2	3	4

Supervisor/instructor signature ________________ Date ________

▶ TASK Inspect, remove, and/or replace torsion bars and mounts. MAST 4C8

Time off________

Time on________

Total time________

CDX Tasksheet Number: C194

Vehicle used for this activity:

Year____________ Make______________________________ Model____________________

Odometer__________________________ VIN ______________________________________

1. **Research the disassembly and inspection procedure for the torsion bars and mounts in the appropriate service information.**
   a. **List any precautions:**

   b. **List or print off and attach to this sheet the steps to remove the torsion bar:**

   c. **List the flat rate time to remove and install one torsion bar: ________ hrs**
   d. **Specified ride height: ______________________________**

2. **Have your supervisor/instructor verify your answers.**
   Supervisor's/instructor's initials: ______________________________

3. **Measure and record vehicle ride height. Note your findings here:**

4. **Safely raise and support the vehicle.**

5. **Following the specified procedure outlined in the service information, remove one torsion bar from the vehicle. List your observation(s):**
   a. **Torsion bar:**

   b. **Mounts:**

   c. **Height-adjustment mechanism:**

   d. **Bushing(s):**

6. **Determine any necessary action(s):**

7. **Have your instructor verify the removal and disassembly of the torsion bar, and check your observations and necessary actions.**
   Supervisor's/instructor's initials: ________________

8. **Reinstall the torsion bar according to the manufacturer's procedure and precautions. Be careful when installing and compressing the spring as it can cause severe injury or death if installed improperly.**

9. **Torque all retaining bolts to the manufacturer's specifications.**

10. **Following the manufacturer's procedure, adjust the ride height of the vehicle to meet specifications.**

11. **Inspect the suspension for any loose fasteners, improperly installed components, etc. List your observations here:**

12. **Determine any necessary action(s):**

13. **Have your supervisor/instructor verify satisfactory completion of this procedure, any observations found, and any necessary action(s) recommended.**

Performance Rating

CDX Tasksheet Number: C194

☐	☐	☐	☐	☐
0	1	2	3	4

Supervisor/instructor signature ______________________________ Date ____________

▶ TASK Perform prealignment inspection and measure vehicle ride height; determine needed action.

Time off________________

Time on________________

Total time________________

CDX Tasksheet Number: C617

1. **Research the prealignment process for this vehicle in the appropriate service information.**
   a. **List the ride-height specifications:**

   b. **Can the ride height be manually adjusted on this vehicle?**
      Yes: ________ No: ________
      i. **If yes, what is the specified adjustment procedure?**

   c. **List the specified tire size: ________________________________**
   d. **List the specified tire pressure(s): ________________________ psi/kPa**
   e. **List any other manufacturer-specified checks:**

2. **Following the specified procedure, inspect the vehicle.**
   a. **Is the vehicle abnormally loaded? Yes: ________ No: ________**
   b. **Are the specified tires installed on the vehicle?**
      Yes: ________ No: ________
   c. **List the condition and wear of each tire as you inflate the tires to proper pressure:**

      Left front: (Initial psi): ____________ psi; Condition:____________________
      Right front: (Initial psi): ____________ psi; Condition:____________________
      Right rear: (Initial psi): ____________ psi; Condition:____________________
      Left rear: (Initial psi): ____________ psi; Condition:____________________
   d. **Does the vehicle meet the specified ride height?**
      Yes: ________ No: ________
   e. **List the results of other specified checks:**

3. **Perform any necessary action(s) and list your results:**

4. **Does the vehicle meet the prealignment inspection requirements for an alignment? Yes: ________ No: ________**

5. **Have your supervisor/instructor verify satisfactory completion of this procedure, any observations found, and any necessary action(s) recommended.**

Performance Rating

CDX Tasksheet Number: C617

☐	☐	☐	☐	☐
0	1	2	3	4

Supervisor/instructor signature ______________________________ Date ________

▶ TASK Prepare vehicle for wheel alignment on alignment machine; perform four-wheel alignment by checking and adjusting front and rear wheel caster, camber, and toe as required; center steering wheel.

MAST 4E3

Time off________

Time on________

Total time________

CDX Tasksheet Number: C618

1. **Prepare the vehicle for wheel alignment on the alignment machine.**

2. **Perform four-wheel alignment measurements and list the following readings:**
   Front wheels:
   a. **Caster: LF:** ________ **RF:** ________ **Specs:** ________
   b. **Cross caster: Measured:** ________ **Specs:** ________
   c. **Camber: LF:** ________ **RF:** ________ **Specs:** ________
   d. **Cross camber: Measured:** ________ **Specs:** ________
   e. **Toe: LF:** ________ **RF:** ________ **Specs:** ________
   f. **Total toe: Measured:** ________ **Specs:** ________

   Rear wheels:
   g. **Caster: LF:** ________ **RF:** ________
   Specs: ________
   h. **Cross caster: Measured:** ________ **Specs:** ________
   i. **Camber: LF:** ________ **RF:** ________ **Specs:** ________
   j. **Cross camber: Measured:** ________ **Specs:** ________
   k. **Toe: LF:** ________ **RF:** ________ **Specs:** ________
   l. **Total toe: Measured:** ________ **Specs:** ________

3. **Determine any necessary action(s):**

4. **Have your supervisor/instructor verify satisfactory completion of this procedure, any observations found, and any necessary action(s) recommended.**

Performance Rating

CDX Tasksheet Number: C618

0	1	2	3	4
☐	☐	☐	☐	☐

Supervisor/instructor signature ________ Date ________

▶ TASK Reset steering angle sensor.

MAST 4E9

Time off________

Time on________

Total time________

CDX Tasksheet Number: C940

1. **Research the steering angle sensor reset procedure for this vehicle in the appropriate service information.**
   a. **List, or print out and attach, the steps to reset the sensor:**

   b. **List any special tools required for this procedure:**

2. **If possible, list the current steering angle:** ____________________

3. **Following the specified procedure, reset the steering angle sensor. List any observation(s):**

4. **List the final steering angle:** ____________________

5. **Have your supervisor/instructor verify satisfactory completion of this procedure, any observations found, and any necessary action(s) recommended.**

Performance Rating

CDX Tasksheet Number: C940

0	1	2	3	4
☐	☐	☐	☐	☐

Supervisor/instructor signature ____________________ Date __________

▶ TASK Check toe-out-on-turns (turning radius); determine needed action.

MAST
4E4

Time off______________

Time on______________

Total time______________

CDX Tasksheet Number: C213

1. **Following the manufacturer's procedure, measure toe-out-on-turns.**
   a. **LF wheel set at: ________________ degrees**
   b. **RF wheel measures: ________________ degrees**
   c. **RF wheel set at: ________________ degrees**
   d. **LF wheel measures: ________________ degrees**

2. **Determine any necessary action(s):**

3. **Have your supervisor/instructor verify satisfactory completion of this procedure, any observations found, and any necessary action(s) recommended.**

Performance Rating

CDX Tasksheet Number: C213

0	1	2	3	4
☐	☐	☐	☐	☐

Supervisor/instructor signature ________________________________ Date ______________

▶ TASK Check steering axis inclination (SAI) and included angle; determine needed action.

MAST 4E5

Time off________

Time on________

Total time________

CDX Tasksheet Number: C214

1. **Following the manufacturer's procedure, measure SAI (steering axis inclination) and included angle.**
   a. **SAI: LF:** ______________ **Specs:** ______________
   b. **SAI: RF:** ______________ **Specs:** ______________
   c. **Included angle: LF:** ______________ **Specs:** ______________
   d. **Included angle: RF:** ______________ **Specs:** ______________

2. **Determine any necessary action(s):**

3. **Have your supervisor/instructor verify satisfactory completion of this procedure, any observations found, and any necessary action(s) recommended.**

Performance Rating

CDX Tasksheet Number: C214

☐	☐	☐	☐	☐
0	1	2	3	4

Supervisor/instructor signature ______________________________ Date ____________

▶ TASK Check rear wheel thrust angle; determine needed action.

MAST 4E6

Time off________

Time on________

Total time________

CDX Tasksheet Number: C216

1. **Following the manufacturer's procedure, measure the rear wheel thrust angle.**
    a. **Manufacturer's specifications:** ______________________________
    b. **Measured thrust angle:** ______________________________

2. **Determine any necessary action(s):**

3. **Have your supervisor/instructor verify satisfactory completion of this procedure, any observations found, and any necessary action(s) recommended.**

Performance Rating

CDX Tasksheet Number: C216

0	1	2	3	4
☐	☐	☐	☐	☐

Supervisor/instructor signature ______________________________ Date ____________

▶ TASK Check for front wheel setback; determine needed action. MAST 4E7

CDX Tasksheet Number: C217

Time off________

Time on________

Total time________

1. **Following the manufacturer's procedure, check for front wheel setback.**
   a. **Manufacturer's specifications:** ____________________
   b. **Measured setback:** ____________________

2. **Determine any necessary action(s):**

3. **Have your supervisor/instructor verify all of your measurements and necessary actions for all of the previous tasks. Get permission to perform the necessary action(s). Supervisor's/instructor's initials:** ____________________

4. **Perform all of the adjustments necessary for a four-wheel alignment as listed in the previous tasks.**

5. **When finished, remeasure all alignment angles to make sure they are within specifications.**

6. **List or print off and attach to this sheet the post-alignment measurements. Front wheels:**
   a. **Caster: LF:** __________ **RF:** __________ **Specs:** __________
   b. **Cross caster: Measured:** __________ **Specs:** __________
   c. **Camber: LF:** __________ **RF:** __________ **Specs:** __________
   d. **Cross camber: Measured:** __________ **Specs:** __________
   e. **Toe: LF:** __________ **RF:** __________ **Specs:** __________
   f. **Total toe: Measured:** __________ **Specs:** __________

   Rear wheels:
   a. **Caster: LF:** __________ **RF:** __________ **Specs:** __________
   b. **Cross caster: Measured:** __________ **Specs:** __________
   c. **Camber: LF:** __________ **RF:** __________ **Specs:** __________
   d. **Cross camber: Measured:** __________ **Specs:** __________
   e. **Toe: LF:** __________ **RF:** __________ **Specs:** __________
   f. **Total toe: Measured:** __________ **Specs:** __________

   Toe-out-on-turns:
   a. **LF wheel set at:** __________ **degrees**
   b. **RF wheel measures:** __________ **degrees**
   c. **RF wheel set at:** __________ **degrees**
   d. **LF wheel measures:** __________ **degrees**

7. **SAI:** __________ **degrees**

8. **Included angle:** __________ **degrees**

9. **Rear wheel thrust angle:** __________ **degrees**

10. List the measurement(s) for front wheel setback: ___________

11. Is the steering wheel centered? Yes: ________ No: ________

12. Do all the angles meet the manufacturer's specifications?
Yes: ________ No: ________

13. Determine any further necessary action(s), such as resetting the steering angle sensor:

14. Inspect the vehicle for any loose or missing fasteners or improper repairs. List your observation(s):

15. Have your supervisor/instructor verify satisfactory completion of this procedure, any observations found, and any necessary action(s) recommended.

Performance Rating

CDX Tasksheet Number: C217

☐	☐	☐	☐	☐
0	1	2	3	4

Supervisor/instructor signature ______________________ Date ________

▶ TASK Check front and/or rear cradle (subframe) alignment; determine needed action.

MAST 4E8

Time off__________

Time on__________

Total time__________

CDX Tasksheet Number: C795

Vehicle used for this activity:

Year __________ Make ____________________ Model________________

Odometer ____________________ VIN ________________________

1. **Following the manufacturer's procedure, check front and rear cradle alignment.**
   a. **Manufacturer's specifications:**

   b. **Measured cradle alignment:**

2. **Determine any necessary action(s):**

3. **Have your supervisor/instructor verify satisfactory completion of this procedure, any observations found, and any necessary action(s) recommended.**

Performance Rating

CDX Tasksheet Number: C795

0	1	2	3	4
☐	☐	☐	☐	☐

Supervisor/instructor signature ______________________________ Date __________

TASK Research vehicle service information including fluid type, vehicle service history, service precautions, and technical service bulletins.

MAST 5A2

Time off________

Time on________

Total time________

CDX Tasksheet Number: C230

1. **Using the VIN for identification, use the appropriate source to access the vehicle's service history in relation to prior braking system work or customer concerns.**
   a. **List any related repairs/concerns, and their dates:**

   b. **List any service precautions related to brake system diagnosis and repair:**

2. **List the specified type of brake fluid for this vehicle:** ________________

3. **Using the VIN for identification, access any relevant technical service bulletins for the particular vehicle you are working on in relation to braking system updates or other service issues. List related TSBs and their description(s):**

4. **Have your supervisor/instructor verify satisfactory completion of this procedure, any observations found, and any necessary action(s) recommended.**

Performance Rating

CDX Tasksheet Number: C230

0	1	2	3	4
☐	☐	☐	☐	☐

Supervisor/instructor signature ________________ Date ________

▶ TASK Demonstrate the use of the three Cs (concern, cause, and correction). **Additional Task**

Time off________

Time on________

Total time________

CDX Tasksheet Number: N/A

1. **Using the following scenario, write up the three Cs as listed on most repair orders. Assume that the customer authorized the recommended repairs.**
   A vehicle is brought to your shop with a brake concern. The customer tells you that the brakes make a grinding noise that comes from the front wheels when the brakes are applied. The vehicle has been doing this for about two weeks, but the customer was too busy to bring the car in for repairs. You remove the wheels, inspect all of the brakes, and find the following:

   a. **The brake pads on the left front are worn down to metal and have scored the rotor badly. The rotor is worn down to the point that it is 0.043 of an inch under the minimum specified thickness.**
   b. **The right side brake pads are worn well below minimum specifications but have not worn down to metal. The rotor is about 0.040 of an inch thicker than the minimum thickness specified.**
   c. **Both front calipers appear to be original and the pistons do not move as freely as they should; the brake fluid is very dark and dirty.**
   d. **The rear brake shoes are in like-new condition, but wet with brake fluid.**

> **NOTE** Ask your instructor whether you should use a copy of the shop repair order, or the three Cs here, to record this information.

2. **Concern/complaint:**

3. **Cause:**

4. **Correction:**

5. **Other recommended service:**

6. **Have your supervisor/instructor verify satisfactory completion of this procedure, any observations found, and any necessary action(s) recommended.**

Performance Rating

CDX Tasksheet Number: N/A

0	1	2	3	4

Supervisor/instructor signature ______________________ Date ________

▶ TASK Describe the operation of a regenerative braking system. **MAST 5G2**

CDX Tasksheet Number: C950

Time off________

Time on________

Total time________

1. **Research the operation of a regenerative braking system on a vehicle equipped with this system in the appropriate service information.**
    a. **In your own words, write out a summary of how the system operates:**

2. **Have your supervisor/instructor verify satisfactory completion of this procedure, any observations found, and any necessary action(s) recommended.**

Performance Rating

CDX Tasksheet Number: C950

0	1	2	3	4

Supervisor/instructor signature ________ Date ________

▶ TASK Diagnose poor stopping, noise, vibration, pulling, grabbing, dragging, or pedal pulsation concerns; determine needed action.

MAST 5C1

Time off________

Time on________

Total time________

CDX Tasksheet Number: C706

1. **List the drum brake-related customer complaint/concern:**

2. **Research the description and operation of the brake system for this vehicle in the appropriate service information. Also research the drum brake diagnostic procedure and removal/installation procedures.**
    a. **List the possible cause(s) of the complaint/concern:**

3. **With instructor permission, test-drive the vehicle to verify the concern. Be sure to follow all shop policies regarding test drives. List your observations:**

4. **Reflecting back on this job, list the causes of the customer concern as listed at the beginning of this tasksheet:**

5. **Document the correction(s) required to correct the customer concern:**

6. **Did you repair the vehicle? Yes: __________ No: __________**

7. **List any additional necessary action(s):**

8. **Have your supervisor/instructor verify satisfactory completion of this procedure, any observations found, and any necessary action(s) recommended.**

Performance Rating

CDX Tasksheet Number: C706

☐	☐	☐	☐	☐
0	1	2	3	4

Supervisor/instructor signature _______________ Date _______

▶ TASK Install wheel and torque lug nuts.

MAST 5A4

Time off________

Time on________

Total time________

CDX Tasksheet Number: C251

1. **Install the wheel(s), place lug nuts on studs with the proper side facing the wheel, and torque them to proper torque in the specified sequence.**

> **NOTE** The lug nut contact face MUST match the contact face in the wheel. If the wheel contact face is tapered, the lug nut contact face MUST also be tapered to match. If the contact face in the wheel is flat, the contact face of the lug nut MUST be flat. If in doubt about which way the lug nuts should face, ask your instructor.

2. **To what torque did you tighten the lug nuts? ________ ft-lb/ N·m**
3. **Reinstall any wheel covers that have been removed.**
4. **Have your supervisor/instructor feel brake pedal application and determine whether a test drive is necessary to final adjust the brakes and verify satisfactory operation of brakes.**

Performance Rating

CDX Tasksheet Number: C251

☐	☐	☐	☐	☐
0	1	2	3	4

Supervisor/instructor signature ________________ Date ________

▶ TASK Remove, clean, and inspect brake drum; measure brake drum diameter; determine serviceability.

MAST 5C2

Time off_______________

Time on_______________

Total time_______________

CDX Tasksheet Number: C800

1. **Research the description and operation of the brake system for this vehicle in the appropriate service information. Also research the drum brake removal/ installation procedures.**
    a. **Maximum drum diameter: _____________ in/mm**
    b. **Maximum drum out-of-round: _____________ in/mm**
    c. **Minimum lining thickness: (Primary) _____________ in/mm; (Secondary) _____________ in/mm**
    d. **Parking brake adjustment specification: _____________**
    e. **Lug nut torque: _____________ ft-lb/ N·m**
        i. **Draw lug nut-torque pattern:**

2. **Remove the brake drum following the specified procedure, being careful not to disturb any brake dust. Clean the brake drum using equipment/procedures for dealing with asbestos/dust.**

3. **Inspect the drum.**
    a. **Measure and record the diameter: _____________ in/mm**
    b. **Measure and record the amount of out-of-round: _____________ in/mm**

> NOTE Measure in at least three places equally spaced around the drum.

    c. **Hot spots? Yes: _____________ No: _____________**
    d. **Cracks? Yes: _____________ No: _____________**
    e. **Other defects? List if found:**

4. **Based on your observations/measurements, determine any necessary action(s):**

5. **Have your supervisor/instructor verify satisfactory completion of this procedure, any observations found, and any necessary action(s) recommended.**

Performance Rating

CDX Tasksheet Number: C800

0	1	2	3	4

Supervisor/instructor signature _______________ Date _______________

▶ TASK Refinish brake drum and measure final drum diameter; compare to specification.

MAST 5C3

Time off________

Time on________

Total time________

CDX Tasksheet Number: C626

1. **Mount the brake drum on the brake lathe following the brake lathe manufacturer's procedure, and set it up for a cut, BUT DON'T MAKE A CUT!**
2. **Have your instructor verify proper setup. Supervisor/Instructor initials: ________________**
3. **Using the correct equipment and procedure, refinish the brake drum to within allowable tolerances.**
4. **Measure the final drum diameter and note your measurement here: ________________ in/mm**
5. **Calculate the amount of material removed by the refinishing process: ________________ in/mm**
6. **Does the drum meet specifications to be safely put back into service? Yes: ________________ No: ________________**
   a. **Why or why not?**
7. **Have your supervisor/instructor verify satisfactory completion of this procedure, any observations found, and any necessary action(s) recommended.**

Performance Rating

CDX Tasksheet Number: C626

0	1	2	3	4
☐	☐	☐	☐	☐

Supervisor/instructor signature ________________ Date ________

▶ TASK Remove, clean, inspect, and/or replace brake shoes, springs, pins, clips, levers, adjusters/self-adjusters, other related brake hardware, and backing support plates; lubricate and reassemble.

MAST 5C4

Time off________

Time on________

Total time________

CDX Tasksheet Number: C248

1. **Clean brake shoes, hardware, and backing plates using equipment and procedures for dealing with asbestos/dust.**

2. **Disassemble the brake shoes and hardware from the backing plate, being careful not to lose any parts and remembering how they go back together.**
   a. **Measure lining thickness: (Primary) ____________ in/mm; (Secondary) ____________ in/mm**
   b. **Inspect and clean hardware:**
      i. **Springs:**
      Damaged: ____________ **Missing:** ____________
      Weak: ____________ **Okay:** ____________
      ii. **Pins:**
      Damaged: ____________ **Missing:** ____________
      Okay: ____________
      iii. **Levers and adjusters:**
      Damaged: ____________ **Missing:** ____________
      Okay: ____________
      iv. **Backing plate:**
      Damaged: ____________ **Worn:** ____________
      Okay: ____________
      v. **Other hardware:**
      Damaged: ____________ **Missing:** ____________
      Okay: ____________

3. **Determine any necessary action(s):**

4. **Have your instructor initial to verify condition of hardware:** ____________

> **NOTE** Many vehicles use a primary shoe toward the front of the vehicle and a secondary shoe toward the rear of the vehicle. Refer to the manufacturer's procedure to install the shoes, springs, and hardware correctly.

5. **Following the manufacturer's procedure, lightly lubricate the support pads on the backing plate and reassemble the brake assembly (shoes, springs, hardware, etc.).**

> **NOTE** The brake shoe support pads on the backing plate require a thin film of the proper lubricant applied to their contact surface. This will reduce the wear on the backing plate as the side of the brake shoe rubs against the backing plate as the brakes are operated. Lubriplate (or in some cases, antiseize) is commonly used for this purpose. Just make sure that it only goes on light enough so you can see through it. If too much lubricant is used, it can contaminate the brake linings, which can cause the brakes to grab.

6. **Are the springs seated correctly? Yes: ________ No: ________**

7. **Does the self-adjuster operate properly? Yes: ________ No: ________**

8. **List any necessary action(s):**

9. **Have your supervisor/instructor verify satisfactory completion of this procedure, any observations found, and any necessary action(s) recommended.**

Performance Rating

CDX Tasksheet Number: C248

☐	☐	☐	☐	☐
0	1	2	3	4

Supervisor/instructor signature ________________________________ Date ________

▶ TASK Inspect wheel cylinders for leaks and proper operation; remove and replace as needed.

Time off________

Time on________

Total time________

CDX Tasksheet Number: C707

1. **Inspect the wheel cylinder for leaks or damages dust boots. List your observations:**

2. **Place one thumb in each end of the wheel cylinder. Try to move both pistons side-to-side. This will indicate whether the pistons are stuck in their bores. List your observations:**

3. **Remove the wheel cylinder following the specified procedure.**

> NOTE To prevent twisting the brake line, it is common practice to loosen the brake line fitting before unbolting the wheel cylinder from the backing plate.

4. **Ask your instructor if you should disassemble the wheel cylinder. If no, skip to step #4. If yes, disassemble, clean, and inspect the wheel cylinder for damage, wear, or missing pieces.**
   a. **Bore:**
      Damaged: ________ **Okay:** ________
   b. **Pistons:**
      Damaged: ________ **Missing:** ________
      Okay: ________
   c. **Seals:**
      Damaged: ________ **Missing:** ________
      Okay: ________
   d. **Dust boots:**
      Damaged: ________ **Missing:** ________
      Okay: ________
   e. **Spring(s):**
      Damaged: ________ **Missing:** ________
      Okay: ________

5. **List any necessary action(s):**

6. **Have your supervisor/instructor inspect the removed or disassembled wheel cylinder and determine whether it should be rebuilt, replaced with new, or reinstalled:**
   a. **Rebuild: ______________ Replace: ______________**
      Reinstall: ______________ (Choose one, then instructor initial)
   b. **If rebuilding the wheel cylinder, use new seals, dust boots, springs, and expanders.**

7. **Reinstall the wheel cylinder on the backing plate.**

> NOTE It is usually best to start the brake line fitting into the wheel cylinder before bolting the cylinder down. This will allow the threads of the brake line fitting to align with the threads in the wheel cylinder, helping to prevent cross-threading of the parts.

8. **Have your supervisor/instructor verify satisfactory completion of this procedure, any observations found, and any necessary action(s) recommended.**

Performance Rating

CDX Tasksheet Number: C707

☐	☐	☐	☐	☐
0	1	2	3	4

Supervisor/instructor signature ______________________________ Date ______________

▶ TASK Pre-adjust brake shoes and parking brake; install brake drums or drum/hub assemblies and wheel bearings; make final checks and adjustments.

MAST 5C6

Time off________

Time on________

Total time________

CDX Tasksheet Number: C801

1. **Following the specified procedure, pre-adjust the brake shoes and parking brake.**
2. **If this vehicle uses serviceable wheel bearings, see the "Wheel Bearing Service" tasksheet and clean, inspect, service, reinstall, and adjust them according to manufacturer's procedure.**
3. **Install the brake drum.**
   a. **Does the brake drum turn without excessive drag? Yes: ________ No: ________**
   b. **If equipped with adjustable wheel bearings, are they adjusted properly? Yes: ________ No: ________**

> NOTE The brakes may need air bled out of the wheel cylinders if they were removed from the vehicle. If they were, consider bleeding all wheel cylinders once all drums and calipers are back in place. Failure to have all drums and calipers installed could cause damage to the wheel cylinders, calipers, brake shoes, and pads. Ask your instructor if you are unclear about this.

4. **Check to see that the brake master cylinder has the proper amount of brake fluid in it.**
   a. **Is it at the proper level? Yes: ________ No: ________**
      i. **If no, refill with the proper fluid.**
5. **Start the engine and apply the brake pedal (only when all drums and calipers are installed). List brake pedal feel:**
6. **Shut off the engine and check wheel cylinders and brake line fittings for signs of leakage. List your observations:**

7. **Have your supervisor/instructor verify satisfactory completion of this procedure, any observations found, and any necessary action(s) recommended.**

Performance Rating

CDX Tasksheet Number: C801

☐	☐	☐	☐	☐
0	1	2	3	4

Supervisor/instructor signature ______________________ Date __________

▶ TASK Identify and interpret brake system concerns; determine needed action.

MAST 5A1

Time off________

Time on________

Total time________

CDX Tasksheet Number: C229

1. **List the customer concern:**

2. **Research the particular concern in the appropriate service information.**
   a. **List the possible causes:**

3. **Inspect the braking system to determine the cause of the concern, and list the steps you took to determine the fault:**

4. **List the cause of the concern/complaint:**

5. **List the necessary action(s) to correct this fault:**

6. **Have your supervisor/instructor verify satisfactory completion of this procedure, any observations found, and any necessary action(s) recommended.**

Performance Rating

CDX Tasksheet Number: C229

☐	☐	☐	☐	☐
0	1	2	3	4

Supervisor/instructor signature ________________ Date ________

▶ TASK Describe procedure for performing a road test to check brake system operation, including an anti-lock brake system (ABS).

Time off________

Time on________

Total time________

CDX Tasksheet Number: C944

1. **Research the shop policies for performing a road test to check brake system operation. List the shop policies:**

2. **List the precautions that should be taken before road testing brakes:**

3. **List the precautions that should be taken during road testing of brakes, including testing of the ABS:**

4. **Have your supervisor/instructor verify satisfactory completion of this procedure, any observations found, and any necessary action(s) recommended.**

Performance Rating

CDX Tasksheet Number: C944

☐	☐	☐	☐	☐
0	1	2	3	4

Supervisor/instructor signature ____________________ Date ________

▶ TASK Diagnose poor stopping, noise, vibration, pulling, grabbing, dragging, or pulsation concerns; determine needed action.

Time off________

Time on________

Total time________

CDX Tasksheet Number: C708

1. **List the brake-related customer complaints/concerns:**

2. **Research the description and operation of the brake system for this vehicle in the appropriate service information. Also, research the disc brake diagnostic procedure and removal/installation procedures.**
   a. **List the possible cause(s) of the complaint/concern:**

   b. **Minimum brake pad thickness: __________ in/mm**
   c. **Caliper bore-to-piston clearance (maximum): __________ in/mm**
   d. **List specified caliper slide lubricant: __________**
   e. **Caliper bolt torque: __________ ft-lb/ N·m**
   f. **Lug nut torque: __________ ft-lb/ N·m**
   g. **Draw the lug nut torque pattern for this vehicle:**

3. **With instructor permission, test-drive the vehicle to verify the complaint.**

NOTE Be sure to follow all shop policies regarding test drives.

   a. **List your observations:**

4. **Reflecting back on this job, list the cause(s) of the customer concerns as listed at the beginning of this tasksheet:**

5. **Document the correction(s) required to fix the customer concern:**

6. **Did you repair the vehicle? Yes: __________ No: __________**

7. **List any additional necessary action(s):**

8. **Return the vehicle to its beginning condition and return any tools you used to their proper locations.**

9. **Have your supervisor/instructor verify satisfactory completion of this procedure, any observations found, and any necessary action(s) recommended.**

Performance Rating

CDX Tasksheet Number: C708

0	1	2	3	4
☐	☐	☐	☐	☐

Supervisor/instructor signature ______________________________ Date __________

▶ TASK Diagnose poor stopping, pulling, or dragging concerns caused by malfunctions in the hydraulic system; determine needed action.

Time off________

Time on________

Total time________

CDX Tasksheet Number: C236

1. **List the brake-related (hydraulic system) customer complaint or concern:**

2. **Research the particular concern in the appropriate service information. List the possible cause(s):**

3. **With instructor permission, test-drive the vehicle to verify the concern.**

> **NOTE** Be sure to follow all shop policies regarding test drives.

   a. **List your observations:**

4. **Follow the specified procedure to inspect and diagnose the problem. Document the steps you took to determine the cause, and the results of those steps, in the space below:**

5. **List the root cause(s) of the concern(s):**

6. **Determine any necessary action(s):**

7. **Have your supervisor/instructor verify satisfactory completion of this procedure, any observations found, and any necessary action(s) recommended.**

Performance Rating

CDX Tasksheet Number: C236

☐	☐	☐	☐	☐
0	1	2	3	4

Supervisor/instructor signature ____________________ Date __________

▶ TASK Remove and clean caliper assembly; inspect for leaks, damage, and wear; determine needed action.

MAST 5D2

Time off________

Time on________

Total time________

CDX Tasksheet Number: C802

1. **Raise the vehicle and support it properly. Remove the wheel and tire assembly.**
2. **Break loose or open the bleeder screw (then close it) to ensure that it is not seized in place and is able to open. Failure to find this out now could waste a lot of time later trying to repair a bleeder screw that has broken off, if it is seized. Also, if replacing the caliper, it is good practice to bleed all of the old brake fluid out of the brake system at this time, so that old brake fluid isn't run though the new caliper.**
3. **Remove the caliper assembly from its mountings, following the specified procedure. If removing the caliper completely, be careful not to lose the two copper sealing rings when removing the brake line, if applicable.**
4. **Inspect the caliper for leaks or damage, being careful to avoid dislodging brake dust, which may contain asbestos. List your observations:**
   a. **Leaks:**

   b. **Damage/wear:**
5. **Following the specified procedure, clean the caliper assembly.**
6. **Based on your observations, determine any necessary action(s):**
7. **Have your supervisor/instructor verify satisfactory completion of this procedure, any observations found, and any necessary action(s) recommended.**

Performance Rating

CDX Tasksheet Number: C802

☐	☐	☐	☐	☐
0	1	2	3	4

Supervisor/instructor signature ________________ Date ________

▶ TASK Inspect caliper mounting and slides/pins for proper operation, wear, and damage; determine needed action.

MAST 5D3

Time off________

Time on________

Total time________

CDX Tasksheet Number: C803

1. **Following the specified procedure, clean the caliper mounts and slides/pins.**
2. **Inspect the caliper mounts, slides/pins, and any threads for operation, wear, and damage. List your observations:**
   a. **Operation:**
   b. **Wear:**
   c. **Damage:**
3. **Based on your observations, determine any necessary action(s):**
4. **Have your supervisor/instructor verify satisfactory completion of this procedure, any observations found, and any necessary action(s) recommended.**

Performance Rating

CDX Tasksheet Number: C803

0	1	2	3	4

Supervisor/instructor signature ________ Date ________

TASK Check brake pad wear indicator; determine needed action.

MAST 5D12

Time off_______

Time on_______

Total time_______

CDX Tasksheet Number: C632

1. **List what type of wear indicator system this vehicle uses:**

2. **Check the brake pad wear indicator. How much brake pad thickness remains until the indicator contacts the surface of the rotor?**

   Note your measurement: ___________________ in/mm

3. **Determine any necessary action(s):**

4. **Have your supervisor/instructor verify satisfactory completion of this procedure, any observations found, and any necessary action(s) recommended.**

Performance Rating

CDX Tasksheet Number: C632

☐	☐	☐	☐	☐
0	1	2	3	4

Supervisor/instructor signature _______________________ Date _________

▶ TASK Remove, inspect, and/or replace brake pads and retaining hardware; determine needed action.

MAST 5D4

Time off__________

Time on__________

Total time__________

CDX Tasksheet Number: C627

1. **Remove and inspect pads and retaining hardware in accordance with the correct procedure.**
2. **Measure the remaining brake pad thickness: ________________ in/mm**
3. **Inspect the brake pads and retaining hardware. List condition(s) found:**
4. **Determine any necessary action(s):**
5. **Have your supervisor/instructor verify satisfactory completion of this procedure, any observations found, and any necessary action(s) recommended.**

> **NOTE** Because you have the rotor exposed, go to the "Rotor Inspection and Service" tasksheet and complete the tasks listed there. This will save you time and effort. Return to this tasksheet and pick up here once you are done with the rotor.

Performance Rating

CDX Tasksheet Number: C627

☐	☐	☐	☐	☐
0	1	2	3	4

Supervisor/instructor signature ____________________ Date __________

▶ TASK Lubricate and reinstall caliper, brake pads, and related hardware; seat brake pads and inspect for leaks.

MAST 5D5

Time off______

Time on______

Total time______

CDX Tasksheet Number: C805

1. **Make sure the rotor has been properly installed on the hub/spindle.**
2. **Reassemble the pads, hardware, and caliper on caliper mounts using the specified lubricant.**

> **NOTE** Torque all bolts to specified torque.

4. **If removed, reinstall the brake line fittings using two copper washers (if equipped). Place one between the brake line fitting and the head of the banjo bolt and the other between the brake line fitting and the caliper.**

> **NOTE** Before performing the next step, ensure that all brake assemblies are completely reassembled, including all brake drums. This will prevent damage to wheel cylinders, brake shoes, and pads.

5. **Seat the pads by applying the brake pedal several times. This will force the brake caliper pistons to adjust to the proper clearance for proper brake application.**

> **NOTE** Failure to perform this step could lead to no brake application when the vehicle is first moved.

6. **If the brake pedal is spongy, you will need to bleed the brakes of any trapped air in the system. See the appropriate CDX tasksheet for guidance.**
7. **If the brake pedal is firm and does not sink over time, there could still be a small leak that would cause a brake failure at some point in time. Inspect the system for any brake fluid leaks, no matter how small; if found, inform your supervisor/instructor.**
    a. **Are there any leaks in the system? Yes: ______ No: ______**
    b. **If yes, where?**
8. **Have your supervisor/instructor verify satisfactory completion of this procedure, any observations found, and any necessary action(s) recommended.**

Performance Rating

CDX Tasksheet Number: C805

☐	☐	☐	☐	☐
0	1	2	3	4

Supervisor/instructor signature ______ Date ______

▶ TASK Retract and readjust caliper piston on an integrated parking brake system.

MAST 5D10

Time off__________

Time on__________

Total time__________

CDX Tasksheet Number: C631

1. **Research the proper method of retracting and readjusting the caliper piston on an integrated parking brake system in the appropriate service information. List any precautions below.**

2. **Following the recommended process, retract the caliper piston. Instructor initials: ____________________**

3. **Reinstall the caliper and readjust the caliper piston. Instructor initials: ____________________**

4. **Determine any necessary action(s):**

5. **Have your supervisor/instructor verify satisfactory completion of this procedure, any observations found, and any necessary action(s) recommended.**

Performance Rating

CDX Tasksheet Number: C631

0	1	2	3	4
☐	☐	☐	☐	☐

Supervisor/instructor signature ____________________ Date __________

▶ TASK Install wheel and torque lug nuts.

MAST 5A4

Time off________

Time on________

Total time________

CDX Tasksheet Number: C251

1. **Install the wheel(s), place lug nuts on studs with the proper side facing the wheel, and torque them to proper torque in the specified sequence.**

> **NOTE** The lug nut contact face MUST match the contact face in the wheel. If the wheel contact face is tapered, the lug nut contact face MUST also be tapered to match. If the contact face in the wheel is flat, the contact face of the lug nut MUST be flat. If in doubt about which way the lug nuts should face, ask your instructor.

2. **To what torque did you tighten the lug nuts? ________________ ft-lb/ N·m**

3. **Reinstall any wheel covers that have been removed.**

4. **Have your supervisor/instructor feel brake pedal application and determine whether a test drive is necessary to final adjust the brakes and verify satisfactory operation of brakes.**

Performance Rating

CDX Tasksheet Number: C251

0	1	2	3	4

Supervisor/instructor signature ______________________________ Date __________

▶ TASK Clean and inspect rotor and mounting surface; measure rotor thickness, thickness variation, and lateral runout; determine needed action.

MAST 5D6

Time off________

Time on________

Total time________

CDX Tasksheet Number: C628

1. **Research rotor inspection, refinishing, removal, and installation procedure in the appropriate service information. Follow all directions.**
   a. **Minimum rotor thickness: ____________ in/mm**
   b. **Maximum thickness variation: ____________ in/mm**
   c. **Maximum lateral runout: ____________ in/mm**

2. **If you haven't already done so, remove the caliper assembly, brake pads, and any hardware following the manufacturer's procedure.**

3. **Clean the rotor with approved asbestos removal equipment.**

4. **Inspect/measure the rotor for the following:**
   a. **Hard spots/hot spots: Yes: ____________ No: ____________**
   b. **Cracks: Yes: ____________ No: ____________**
   c. **Rotor thickness: ____________ in/mm**
   d. **Thickness variation (maximum variation) (check in 6-8 places): ____________ in/mm**
   e. **Lateral runout: ____________ in/mm**
   f. **Is the rotor machinable? Yes: ____________ No: ____________**

5. **Determine any necessary action(s):**

6. **Have your supervisor/instructor verify satisfactory completion of this procedure, any observations found, and any necessary action(s) recommended.**

> NOTE If you are refinishing this rotor on the vehicle, skip down to task C629. Refinish rotor on vehicle; measure final rotor thickness and compare with specifications. If you are refinishing this rotor off the vehicle, continue on to the next task.

Performance Rating

CDX Tasksheet Number: C628

☐	☐	☐	☐	☐
0	1	2	3	4

Supervisor/instructor signature ____________________ Date ____________

▶ TASK Remove and reinstall/replace rotor. **MAST 5D7**

Time off________

Time on________

Total time________

CDX Tasksheet Number: C806

1. **Remove the rotor following the specified procedure.**
2. **Now would be a good time to inspect the rotor, if you haven't already, and consider refinishing it. Ask your supervisor/instructor if you are to inspect and/or refinish the rotor. If so, proceed to task C630.**
3. **If you are to reinstall this rotor, have your supervisor/instructor confirm removal. Supervisor's/instructor's initials: ________________**
4. **When appropriate (most likely after refinishing), reinstall the rotor according to the manufacturer's recommendations.**
5. **If you had to remove the wheel bearing during disassembly, have your supervisor/instructor verify proper adjustment of the bearings.**
    a. **Supervisor's/instructor's initials: ________________**
6. **Have your supervisor/instructor verify satisfactory completion of this procedure, any observations found, and any necessary action(s) recommended.**

> **NOTE** If you came to this tasksheet from the "Disc Brake Inspection and Service" tasksheet, return to that tasksheet and continue where you left off.

Performance Rating

CDX Tasksheet Number: C806

☐	☐	☐	☐	☐
0	**1**	**2**	**3**	**4**

Supervisor/instructor signature ________________________ Date ________

▶ TASK Refinish rotor on vehicle; measure final rotor thickness and compare with specification.

MAST 5D8

Time off_______________

Time on_______________

Total time_______________

CDX Tasksheet Number: C629

1. **Set up the on-car brake lathe following the manufacturer's procedure, ready to make a cut (but don't yet).**
2. **Measure or list the existing rotor thickness: ____________ in/mm**
3. **Have your instructor verify proper setup and initial here: ____________**
4. **Using the correct procedure, refinish the brake rotor to within allowable tolerances. If necessary, give the rotor a non-directional finish using sandpaper or a sanding disc.**
5. **Measure the refinished rotor thickness: ____________ in/mm**
6. **Calculate the amount of material that was removed: ____________ in/mm**
7. **Is the rotor fit for return to service? Yes: ____________ No: ____________**
8. **Determine any necessary action(s):**
9. **Have your supervisor/instructor verify satisfactory completion of this procedure, any observations found, and any necessary action(s) recommended.**

Performance Rating

CDX Tasksheet Number: C629

☐	☐	☐	☐	☐
0	1	2	3	4

Supervisor/instructor signature ________________________________ Date ____________

▶ TASK Refinish rotor off vehicle; measure final rotor thickness and compare with specification.

MAST 5D9

Time off__________

Time on__________

Total time__________

CDX Tasksheet Number: C630

1. **Mount the rotor on the brake lathe following the manufacturer's procedure and set it up, ready to make a cut (but don't yet).**
2. **Measure or list the existing rotor thickness: __________ in/mm**
3. **Have your instructor verify proper set-up and initial here:**
4. **Using the correct procedure, refinish the brake rotor to within allowable tolerances.**
5. **Give the rotor a non-directional finish using sandpaper or an appropriate sanding wheel.**
6. **Measure the refinished rotor thickness: __________ in/mm**
7. **Calculate the amount of material that was removed: __________ in/mm**
8. **Is the rotor fit for return to service? Yes: __________ No: __________**
9. **Determine any necessary action(s):**
10. **Have your supervisor/instructor verify satisfactory completion of this procedure, any observations found, and any necessary action(s) recommended.**

> **NOTE** If the rotor is serviceable, skip down to task C806: Remove and reinstall/replace rotor.

Performance Rating

CDX Tasksheet Number: C630

0	1	2	3	4
☐	☐	☐	☐	☐

Supervisor/instructor signature ____________________ Date __________

▶ TASK Inspect and replace wheel studs.

MAST 5F8

Time off________

Time on________

Total time________

CDX Tasksheet Number: C274

1. **Research the wheel stud removal and installation procedure in the appropriate service manual. Follow all directions carefully.**
   a. **There are generally two standard procedures for replacing wheel studs. One is to remove the hub from the vehicle and use a hydraulic press to remove and install the studs. The other is to use a hammer to drive out the old stud, then use washers and the flat side of the lug nut to draw the new stud into the hub. Which method does the service manual describe for this vehicle?** ________________
   b. **List any special tools or procedures for this task:**

   c. **Lug nut torque:** ________________ **ft-lb/ N·m**

2. **Safely raise the vehicle on a hoist. Check to see that the vehicle is secure on the hoist.**

3. **Remove the wheel assembly and inspect the lug nuts and wheel studs. List your observations and any necessary actions:**

4. **Have your supervisor/instructor verify your observations. Supervisor/ instructor's initials:** ________________

5. **Remove the damaged wheel stud/s from the hub, being careful to follow the specified procedure. List your observations:**

6. **Have your supervisor/instructor verify removal. Supervisor/instructor's initials:** ________________

7. **Install a new wheel stud/s in the hub, following the specified procedure. Make sure the stud is fully seated in the hub. List your observations:**

8. **Have your supervisor/instructor verify the installation. Supervisor/instructor's initials: ______________________**

> **NOTE** If you came to this tasksheet from the "Disc Brake Inspection and Service" tasksheet, return to that tasksheet and continue where you left off.

9. **Reinstall the hub on the vehicle if it was removed. Reinstall the wheel assembly. Torque lug nuts to proper torque.**

10. **Have your supervisor/instructor verify satisfactory completion of this procedure, any observations found, and any necessary action/s recommended.**

Performance Rating

CDX Tasksheet Number: C274

☐	☐	☐	☐	☐
0	1	2	3	4

Supervisor/instructor signature ______________________________ Date __________

TASK Describe the importance of operating vehicle to burnish/break in replacement brake pads according to manufacturer's recommendations.

MAST 5D12

Time off________

Time on________

Total time________

CDX Tasksheet Number: C948

1. **Research the brake pad burnishing/break in process for the vehicle you are working on, in the appropriate service information. List the process here (or print off and attach to this sheet):**

2. **Describe in your own words why it is important to properly burnish/break in brake pads after installation:**

3. **Have your supervisor/instructor verify satisfactory completion of this procedure, any observations found, and any necessary action(s) recommended.**

Performance Rating

CDX Tasksheet Number: C948

0	1	2	3	4

Supervisor/instructor signature ________________ Date ________

▶ TASK Identify components of the brake power assist system (vacuum and hydraulic); check vacuum supply (manifold or auxiliary pump) to vacuum-type power booster.

MAST 5E2

Time off__________

Time on__________

Total time__________

CDX Tasksheet Number: C808

1. **Research the components of the brake power assist system in the appropriate service information.**

2. **Identify and list the type of power assist system:**

   ____

3. **If the vehicle is equipped with vacuum-type power assist, complete the following procedure:**

   a. **Following the specified procedure with the engine running, check the vacuum supply at the brake power booster.**

      i. **List the vacuum reading obtained:**

         ____

   b. **Does this meet the specification requirements for this vehicle?**
      Yes: __________ **No:** __________

      i. **If no, determine the cause(s) of the low vacuum reading and list the condition(s) found.**

> **NOTE** This could be caused by a leak in the system or an engine mechanical/tune-up problem if manifold vacuum is used. Find the specific cause.

4. **Determine necessary action(s):**

5. **Remove the vacuum gauge and reinstall the check valve in the booster.**

6. **Have your supervisor/instructor verify satisfactory completion of this procedure, any observations found, and any necessary action(s) recommended.**

Performance Rating

CDX Tasksheet Number: C808

☐	☐	☐	☐	☐
0	1	2	3	4

Supervisor/instructor signature ____________________ Date __________

▸ TASK Select, handle, store, and fill brake fluids to proper level; use proper fluid type per manufacturer specification.

MAST 5B9

Time off________

Time on________

Total time________

CDX Tasksheet Number: C239

1. **Research the specified brake fluid and the bleeding/flushing procedure for this vehicle using the appropriate service information.**
   a. **Specified fluid:**________
   b. **Bleeding/flushing sequence:**________
   c. **Bleeding/flushing precautions:**

2. **Locate the master cylinder reservoir.**
   a. **List the level of the brake fluid:**________

> **NOTE** If the brake fluid is below the minimum level, it could mean there is a leak in the system or the disc brake pads are worn. Investigate these possibilities and report them to your supervisor/instructor.

3. **If appropriate, add the appropriate type of brake fluid to the master cylinder reservoir to bring it to the full mark.**

4. **Knowledge Check: What precautions should be taken when brake fluid is stored?**

5. **Knowledge Check: List the different types of brake fluid available:**

6. **Have your supervisor/instructor verify satisfactory completion of this procedure, any observations found, and any necessary action(s) recommended.**

Performance Rating

CDX Tasksheet Number: C239

☐	☐	☐	☐	☐
0	1	2	3	4

Supervisor/instructor signature ________ Date ________

▶ TASK Test brake fluid for contamination. **MAST 5B13**

Time off________

Time on________

Total time________

CDX Tasksheet Number: C625

1. **Test the fluid using one of the following procedures:**
    a. **DVOM/DMM–Galvanic Reaction Test**
        i. **Remove the master cylinder cap.**
        ii. **Set the DVOM/DMM to DC volts.**
        iii. **Place the red voltmeter lead in the reservoir brake fluid.**
        iv. **Place the black lead on the metal housing of the master cylinder.**
        v. **List the voltage reading obtained:________________ V**

> **NOTE** If reading is above 0.3V, this indicates a galvanic reaction and means there is an unacceptable level of moisture in the brake fluid.

Determine any necessary actions:

    b. **Brake Fluid Tester**
        i. **Follow the directions for the tester you have and test the brake fluid.**
        ii. **List your findings:**

    c. **Brake Fluid Test Strip**
        i. **Follow the directions for the test strip you have and test the brake fluid.**
        ii. **List your findings:**

2. **Have your supervisor/instructor verify satisfactory completion of this procedure, any observations found, and any necessary action(s) recommended.**

Performance Rating

CDX Tasksheet Number: C625

☐	☐	☐	☐	☐
0	1	2	3	4

Supervisor/instructor signature ________________ Date ________

▶ TASK Bleed and/or flush brake system.

MAST 5B12

Time off________

Time on________

Total time________

CDX Tasksheet Number: C705

1. **Which method of bleeding/flushing will you use?**________________
2. **In what order will you be bleeding the brakes?**________________
3. **Remove all old brake fluid from the master cylinder reservoir using the suction gun. Dispose of the fluid properly.**
4. **Refill the master cylinder reservoir using the specified brake fluid.**
5. **Using the appropriate equipment, bleed/flush each brake assembly until clean fluid comes out, making sure you keep the master cylinder reservoir from running low on fluid. Carefully tighten the bleeder screw and replace the bleeder screw dust cap when each wheel assembly is finished.**
   a. **List the condition of the removed fluid:**
6. **Start the engine and apply the brakes to make sure the pedal is still firm. List the pedal feel:**________________
7. **Refill the master cylinder reservoir to the proper level.**
8. **List any necessary action(s):**
9. **Return the vehicle to its beginning condition and return any tools you used to their proper locations.**
10. **Have your supervisor/instructor verify satisfactory completion of this procedure, any observations found, and any necessary action(s) recommended.**

Performance Rating

CDX Tasksheet Number: C705

☐	☐	☐	☐	☐
0	1	2	3	4

Supervisor/instructor signature ________________ Date ________

▶ TASK Measure brake pedal height, travel, and free play (as applicable); determine needed action.

MAST 5B2

Time off________

Time on________

Total time________

CDX Tasksheet Number: C622

1. **Research the description and operation of the brake system for this vehicle in the appropriate service information. Also research the master cylinder diagnostic procedure and removal/installation procedures. Check off the systems in the list below that this vehicle is equipped with:**
   a. **Power assist: Yes: ________ No: ________**
   b. **ABS: Yes: ________ No: ________**
   c. **Four-wheel ABS: Yes: ________ No: ________**
   d. **Rear-wheel ABS: Yes: ________ No: ________**
   e. **Traction control: Yes: ________ No: ________**
   f. **Front-/rear-split hydraulic system: Yes: ________ No: ________**
   g. **Diagonal-split hydraulic system: Yes: ________ No: ________**
   h. **Brake pedal height: ________ in/mm**
   i. **Brake pedal free play: ________ in/mm**
   j. **Brake pedal reserve height: ________ in/mm**

2. **Brake pedal height**
   a. **Following the service procedure, measure the brake pedal height. Record your readings here: ________ in/mm**
   b. **Within specifications? Yes: ________ No: ________**
   c. **If not as specified, determine any necessary actions:**

3. **Reserve pedal height/pedal travel**
   a. **Following the service procedure, start the vehicle and apply the brake pedal with moderate foot pressure. Measure the reserve pedal height/pedal travel and record the measurement: ________ in/mm**
   b. **If not as specified, determine any necessary actions:**

4. **Brake pedal free play**
   a. **Following the service procedure, measure the brake pedal free play and record the measurement here: ________ in/mm**
   b. **Within specifications? Yes: ________ No: ________**
   c. **If not as specified, determine any necessary actions:**

5. **Have your supervisor/instructor verify satisfactory completion of this procedure, any observations found, and any necessary action(s) recommended.**

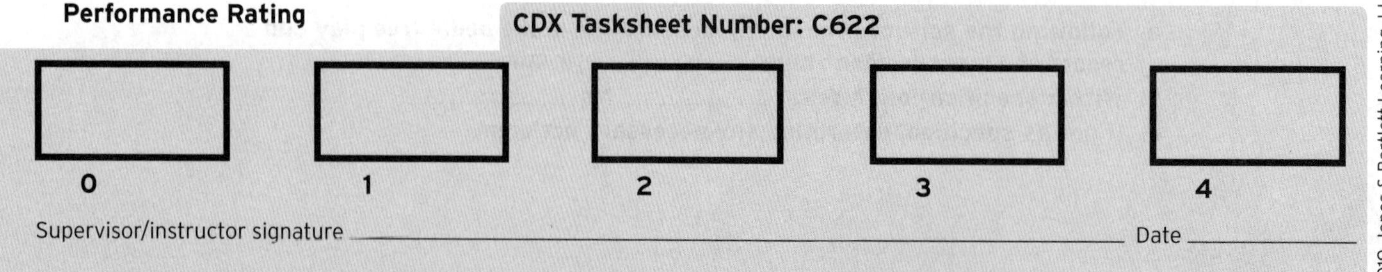

▶ TASK Check brake pedal travel with, and without, engine running to verify proper power booster operation.

MAST 5E1

Time off________

Time on________

Total time________

CDX Tasksheet Number: C807

1. **Research the power booster description, operation, and testing procedure in the appropriate service information.**
   a. **Type of vacuum supply used: Manifold: ________ Auxiliary pump: ________**
   b. **Minimum vacuum at power booster: ________ in.hg**
   c. **Minimum time power booster should hold vacuum: ________ minutes**

2. **Test the ability of the power booster to provide assist.**
   a. **Without starting the vehicle, depress the brake pedal several times. This removes any vacuum from the brake booster. Hold moderate foot pressure on the brake pedal and start the engine.**
      i. **List the brake pedal action:**

      ii. **Is the power booster working properly? Yes: ________ No: ________**
   b. **If the power booster is not working properly, follow the service manual procedure to determine the cause. List any necessary action(s):**

3. **Test the ability of the power booster to hold a vacuum.**
   a. **Without starting the vehicle, depress the brake pedal several times. This removes all vacuum from the brake booster and allows you to feel the brakes without vacuum assist.**
      i. **Approximately how far down does the brake pedal go with moderate foot pressure w/o assist? ________ in/mm**
   b. **With your foot off the brake pedal, start the engine, wait a few seconds, and depress the brake pedal once. This allows you to feel the brakes with power assist. This is how the brake pedal should respond if the power booster is holding vacuum properly.**
      i. **Approximately how far down does the brake pedal travel with moderate foot pressure with assist? ________ in/mm**
   c. **Remove your foot from the brake pedal, turn off the engine, and wait the specified time the power booster should hold vacuum listed above.**

d. After waiting the designated time, and without starting the vehicle, depress the brake pedal once and observe whether the brake pedal travel was the same as in step 3b, indicating the power booster is holding vacuum. List your observations:

e. If the brake pedal responded as in step 3b, no further inspection of the booster is needed.

f. If the brake pedal responded as if it had no vacuum assist (as in 3a), the power booster has a leak, which will need to be diagnosed.

4. Have your supervisor/instructor verify satisfactory completion of this procedure, any observations found, and any necessary action(s) recommended.

Performance Rating

CDX Tasksheet Number: C807

☐	☐	☐	☐	☐
0	1	2	3	4

Supervisor/instructor signature ______________________ Date ________

▶ TASK Diagnose pressure concerns in the brake system using hydraulic principles (Pascal's Law).

MAST
5B1

Time off________

Time on________

Total time________

CDX Tasksheet Number: C894

1. **Have your supervisor/instructor assign you a vehicle found in the service information (you don't need the actual vehicle for this task). Write the details of that vehicle at the top of this page.**

2. **Write out Pascal's Law here:**

3. **Research the description and operation of the vehicle assigned in the appropriate service manual.**

4. **Using Pascal's Law and the service manual, answer the following questions:**
   a. **While braking, how would the vehicle react with a missing left rear wheel cylinder piston seal or caliper seal?**

   b. **While braking, how would the vehicle react with a completely blocked left front flexible brake line?**

   c. **While braking, how would the vehicle react with a torn primary piston pressure seal in the master cylinder?**

5. **Have your supervisor/instructor verify satisfactory completion of this procedure, any observations found, and any necessary action(s) recommended.**

Performance Rating

CDX Tasksheet Number: C894

☐	☐	☐	☐	☐
0	1	2	3	4

Supervisor/instructor signature ______________________________ Date ____________

▶ TASK Check master cylinder for internal/external leaks and proper operation; determine needed action.

MAST 5B3

Time off________

Time on________

Total time________

CDX Tasksheet Number: C704

1. **Research the description and operation of the brake system for this vehicle in the appropriate service information. Also research the master cylinder diagnostic procedure and removal/installation procedures.**
   a. **Master cylinder pushrod length: ____________________ in/mm**
   b. **Master cylinder nut/bolt torque: ____________________ ft/lb or N·m**

2. **Inspect the master cylinder for external leaks.**
   a. **Check the brake fluid level in the reservoir. Record your reading here: ____________________**
   b. **Inspect the master cylinder for obvious signs of leakage. Be sure to check all brake line fittings, sensor connections, reservoir seal(s), and the areas at the rear of the master cylinder near the seal. Also check the inside of the vacuum hose to the power booster.**

> **NOTE** If fluid is found on the inside of the hose, the rear seal in the master cylinder may be leaking fluid into the booster.

   c. **List your observations:**

2. **Check the master cylinder for proper operation.**
   a. **Start the vehicle, apply the brake pedal beginning with a very light pressure, and gradually increasing the pressure. The brake pedal should hold its position with very little travel beyond its applied height. If the pedal continues to sink, the system may have an external or internal leak. Do this test several times with various pedal pressures and time elements. Be sure you hold foot pressure on the system for at least one minute.**
   b. **List your observations:**

3. **Inspect the master cylinder for internal leaks.**
   a. **Remove the master cylinder reservoir cap.**
   b. **Have an assistant apply the brake pedal firmly and hold it. Watch the fluid in the reservoir; it should have an initial spurt of fluid from each of the two compensating ports as the brake pedal is first moved.**

NOTE The brake fluid level should not rise in the reservoir as the brake pedal is held down. If it does, this indicates an internal leak in one or more of the master cylinder seals and it will need to be serviced. On quick take-up type master cylinders, the quick take-up valve vents excess fluid to the rear half of the reservoir.

c. **List your observations:**

4. **Determine any necessary action(s):**

5. **Have your supervisor/instructor verify satisfactory completion of this procedure, any observations found, and any necessary action(s) recommended.**

Performance Rating

CDX Tasksheet Number: C704

0	1	2	3	4

Supervisor/instructor signature _______________ Date _______

▶ TASK Remove, bench bleed, and reinstall master cylinder.

MAST
5B4

Time off________

Time on________

Total time________

CDX Tasksheet Number: C235

1. **Following the specified procedure, perform the following steps to remove the master cylinder.**
   a. **If the master cylinder is being replaced with a new or rebuilt unit, compare the new unit to the old one to verify that it is the correct replacement. If not, inform your supervisor/instructor.**
   b. **Use a suction gun to remove as much brake fluid from the master cylinder reservoir as possible. Do not drip brake fluid on any painted surface of the vehicle.**

> **NOTE** Be careful to avoid getting brake fluid on any painted surface of the vehicle.

   c. **Using flare nut or line wrenches, loosen the brake line fittings. Also use the double wrench method of loosening the fittings if fitted with an adapter. Place a rag under the fittings to catch any leaking brake fluid.**
   d. **Unbolt the master cylinder from the power booster and remove the master cylinder, being careful to avoid getting brake fluid on any painted surface of the vehicle.**

2. **Bench bleed the master cylinder.**

3. **Install the master cylinder, being careful not to cross-thread the fittings.**

> **NOTE** It is good practice to start the fittings by finger before the bolts holding the master cylinder in place are tightened. This helps prevent cross-threading of the fittings in the master cylinder, especially on aluminum master cylinders.

4. **Bleed any remaining air from the hydraulic brake system.**

5. **Verify the correct brake pedal travel and feel.**

6. **Return the vehicle to its beginning condition and return any tools you used to their proper locations.**

7. **Have your supervisor/instructor verify satisfactory completion of this procedure, any observations found, and any necessary action(s) recommended.**

Performance Rating

CDX Tasksheet Number: C235

0	1	2	3	4

Supervisor/instructor signature ________________________________ Date ____________

▶ TASK Measure and adjust master cylinder pushrod length. **MAST 5E5**

Time off________

Time on________

Total time________

CDX Tasksheet Number: C556

1. **Research the specifications and procedure for measuring and adjusting pushrod length in the appropriate service information.**
    a. **Master cylinder pushrod length: ________________ in/mm**
    b. **Master cylinder nut/bolt torque: ________________ ft/lb or N·m**

2. **Measure the pushrod length according to the manufacturer's procedure.**
    a. **List measurement here: ________________ in/mm**

3. **Determine any necessary action(s): Knowledge Check: What would be the customer concern if the pushrod length were too long and caused the master cylinder piston seal to cover one or both of the compensating ports? List your answer.**

4. **Knowledge Check: What would be the customer concern if the pushrod length were substantially shorter than specifications? List your answer.**

5. **Have your supervisor/instructor verify satisfactory completion of this procedure, any observations found, and any necessary action(s) recommended.**

Performance Rating

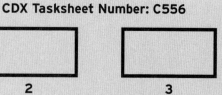

CDX Tasksheet Number: C556

☐	☐	☐	☐	☐
0	1	2	3	4

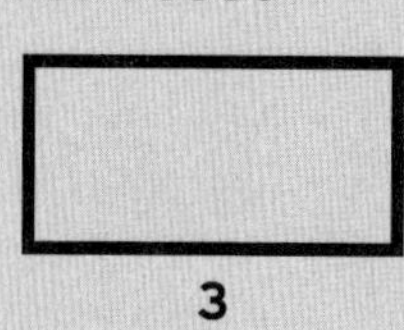
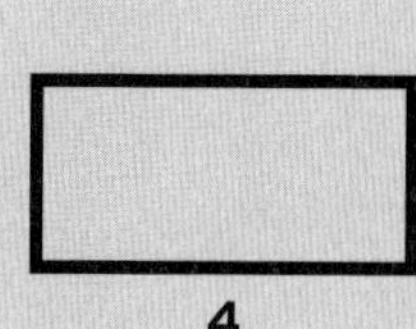

Supervisor/instructor signature ________________________________ Date ________

▶ TASK Inspect vacuum-type power booster unit for leaks; inspect the check valve for proper operation; determine needed action.

MAST 5E3

Time off________

Time on________

Total time________

CDX Tasksheet Number: C809

1. **Test the ability of the power booster to hold a vacuum.**
   a. **Without starting the vehicle, depress the brake pedal several times with moderate pressure.**
   b. **After the vacuum has bled off, approximately how far down does the brake pedal go? ______________________ in/mm**

> NOTE This removes any vacuum from the brake booster and allows you to feel the brakes without vacuum assist.

2. **Start the engine, wait a few seconds, and depress the brake pedal once.**

> NOTE This allows you to feel the brakes with vacuum assist. This is how the brake pedal should respond if the vacuum booster is holding a vacuum properly.

   a. **Approximately how far down does the brake pedal go now? ______________________ in/mm**

3. **Let off the brakes, turn off the engine, and wait the specified time the power booster should hold a vacuum listed previously.**

4. **After waiting the designated time and without starting the vehicle, depress the brake pedal once.**
   a. **Does the brake pedal feel the same as in step 2? Yes: ________ No: ________**

5. **If yes, the power booster and check valve are capable of holding a vacuum, which means the system doesn't have an external vacuum leak (it may still have an internal leak).**

6. **If no, the brake pedal responded as if it had no vacuum assist. Start the vehicle and do the following:**
   a. **Use the electronic stethoscope or the heater hose to listen for vacuum leaks around the outside of the power booster.**
   b. **Listen under the dash at the power booster control valve assembly. List observations found:**

7. Inspect the check valve for proper operation.
    a. Carefully remove the check valve from the power booster, leaving it inserted in the vacuum hose. Start the vehicle and feel whether air is being drawn through the check valve. If it is, this indicates that the valve is not plugged or stuck closed. List observations found:
    b. Reinsert the check valve into the power booster and allow the engine to run for 30 seconds to evacuate the booster. Turn off the engine, wait for the specified minimum time that the power booster should hold a vacuum (listed previously), and then remove the check valve from the booster. There should be a large rush of air into the booster. If there is, the check valve is holding a vacuum and is okay. List observations found:
8. Perform an internal leak test.
    a. Start the engine and let it idle. Apply the brake pedal with moderately firm pressure (20–30 lb) and hold it steady. Without moving your foot, shut off the engine and observe the pedal for approximately one minute. If it stays steady, there are no internal leaks. If the pedal rises, there is an internal leak in either the diaphragm or control valve. List observations found:
9. Based on your observations, determine any necessary actions:
10. Return the vehicle to its beginning condition and return any tools you used to their proper locations.
11. Have your supervisor/instructor verify satisfactory completion of this procedure, any observations found, and any necessary action(s) recommended.

Performance Rating

CDX Tasksheet Number: C809

0	1	2	3	4

Supervisor/instructor signature _______________ Date _______

▶ TASK Inspect and test the hydraulically assisted power brake system for leaks and proper operation; determine needed action.

Time off________

Time on________

Total time________

CDX Tasksheet Number: C581

Vehicle used for this activity:

Year ____________ Make ________________________ Model ________________________

Odometer ____________________ VIN ____

1. **Performance Test: Begin with the vehicle engine off. Apply and release the brake pedal five or six times to discharge the accumulator.**
    a. **Hold the brake pedal down with moderately firm pressure (20-30 lb).**
    b. **Start the engine and observe the brake pedal. If it drops an inch or two, the booster is providing boost. If it does not drop, check the power steering pump belt and power steering pump system. List observations found:**

> NOTE If they are in good condition, consult the service information for further diagnosis.

2. **Accumulator Leak Test: Start the engine, apply the brake pedal, and note the pedal feel and applied height.**
    a. **Release the brake pedal, turn off the engine, and wait at least 10 minutes.**
    b. **Apply the brake pedal with moderately firm pressure (20-30 lb). List observations found:**
    c. **Apply the pedal several more times with the same moderately firm pressure. Each application should result in a higher pedal as the accumulator pressure is released from the booster. If it did, then there are no substantial leaks in the system. If it didn't hold pressure, you will need to perform manufacturer specified tests to determine what is causing the loss in pressure. Determine any necessary action(s):**

3. **Have your supervisor/instructor verify satisfactory completion of this procedure, any observations found, and any necessary action(s) recommended.**

Performance Rating

CDX Tasksheet Number: C581

0	1	2	3	4

Supervisor/instructor signature ______________________ Date ________

TASK Inspect brake lines, flexible hoses, and fittings for leaks, dents, kinks, rust, cracks, bulging, wear, and loose fittings and supports; determine needed action.

MAST 5B6

Time off________

Time on________

Total time________

CDX Tasksheet Number: C237

1. **Safely raise and secure the vehicle on the hoist, then trace all brake lines from the master cylinder to each wheel's brake assembly. Inspect the steel brake lines for the following defects and list each defect's location and cause:**
    a. **Leaks:**
    b. **Dents:**
    c. **Kinks:**
    d. **Rust:**
    e. **Cracks:**
    f. **Wear:**
    g. **Loose fittings or supports:**
2. **Inspect all flexible brake lines for the following defects and list each defect's location and cause:**
    a. **Cracks:**
    b. **Bulging:**
    c. **Wear:**
    d. **Loose fittings or supports:**
3. **Determine any necessary action(s):**
4. **Have your supervisor/instructor verify satisfactory completion of this procedure, any observations found, and any necessary action(s) recommended.**

Performance Rating

CDX Tasksheet Number: C237

0	1	2	3	4
☐	☐	☐	☐	☐

Supervisor/instructor signature ________________ Date ________

▶ TASK Replace brake lines, hoses, fittings, and supports.

MAST 5B7

Time off________

Time on________

Total time________

CDX Tasksheet Number: C623

1. **Safely raise and secure the vehicle on the hoist and, where appropriate, drain the brake line of fluid and safely dispose of it.**

> NOTE You may be able to use a brake pedal depressor to hold down the brake pedal slightly. This will close off the compensating ports in the master cylinder and therefore minimize the amount of fluid draining out of the system. Just remember that the brake lights will stay on continuously while the pedal is depressed.

2. **Carefully remove (using flare nut wrenches) any brake lines, hoses, fittings, and supports that are to be replaced.**
3. **Have your instructor initial to verify removal:** ________
4. **Replace any removed flexible hoses, fittings, and supports in accordance with the service manual procedure.**

> NOTE Be sure to properly route the lines and tighten adequately.

5. **Fill the master cylinder reservoir with the specified fluid.**
6. **Bleed the system in accordance with the recommended procedure.**
7. **Test the system for leaks and integrity. List your observations:**

8. **Have your supervisor/instructor verify satisfactory completion of this procedure, any observations found, and any necessary action(s) recommended.**

Performance Rating

CDX Tasksheet Number: C623

☐	☐	☐	☐	☐
0	1	2	3	4

Supervisor/instructor signature ________ Date ________

▶ TASK Fabricate brake lines using proper material and flaring procedures (double flare and ISO types).

MAST 5B8

Time off________

Time on________

Total time________

CDX Tasksheet Number: C624

1. **Safely raise and secure the vehicle on the hoist and, where appropriate, drain the brake line of fluid and safely dispose of it.**

> **NOTE** You may be able to use a brake pedal depressor to hold down the brake pedal slightly. This will close off the compensating ports in the master cylinder and therefore minimize the amount of fluid draining out of the system. Just remember that the brake lights will stay on continuously while the pedal is depressed.

2. **Carefully remove (using flare nut wrenches) any brake lines and supports that are to be replaced. List the type of flare used on this brake line:**

3. **Fabricate (using the correct equipment and procedure) any brake lines that are to be replaced using proper material and flaring procedures (double flare and ISO types). The old ones can be used for patterns in this regard.**

4. **List the type of tube material used:**________________

5. **Have your instructor inspect the flare. Supervisor's/instructor's initials:**

   ____

6. **Replace any removed brake lines, fittings, and supports in accordance with the service information procedure.**

> **NOTE** Be sure to route the lines properly and tighten adequately.

7. **Fill the master cylinder reservoir with the specified fluid.**

8. **Bleed the system in accordance with the recommended procedure.**

9. **Test the system for leaks and integrity. List your observations:**

10. **Have your supervisor/instructor verify satisfactory completion of this procedure, any observations found, and any necessary action(s) recommended.**

Performance Rating

CDX Tasksheet Number: C624

☐	☐	☐	☐	☐
0	1	2	3	4

Supervisor/instructor signature ________________ Date ________

▶ TASK Identify components of hydraulic brake warning light system.

MAST 5B11

Time off__________

Time on__________

Total time__________

CDX Tasksheet Number: C947

1. **On the appropriate wiring diagram, locate each switch that activates the brake warning light. List those switches here:**

2. **Locate all of the brake warning light switches on the vehicle/simulator. Be prepared to point them out to your supervisor/instructor.**
   a. **Point out the location of the switches to your supervisor/instructor.**

3. **Have your supervisor/instructor verify satisfactory completion of this procedure, any observations found, and any necessary action(s) recommended.**

Performance Rating

CDX Tasksheet Number: C947

0	1	2	3	4

Supervisor/instructor signature ____________________ Date __________

▶ TASK Inspect, test, and/or replace components of brake warning light system.

MAST 5B10

Time off________

Time on________

Total time________

CDX Tasksheet Number: C242

1. **Locate all of the brake warning light switches on the vehicle/simulator. Be prepared to point them out to your supervisor/instructor. Select one of the switches to demonstrate the proper testing procedure. List which switch you are testing:**

2. **Research the diagnosis procedure for the switch being tested.**

3. **Perform the tests on the designated switch and list the steps you took and the results for each:**

4. **Determine any necessary action(s):**

5. **Have your supervisor/instructor verify satisfactory completion of this procedure, any observations found, and any necessary action(s) recommended.**

Performance Rating

CDX Tasksheet Number: C242

0	1	2	3	4
☐	☐	☐	☐	☐

Supervisor/instructor signature ________________ Date ________

▶ TASK Check parking brake operation and indicator light system operation; determine needed action.

Time off________

Time on________

Total time________

CDX Tasksheet Number: C633

1. **Verify that the parking brake is adjusted properly. If necessary, adjust it, being sure to follow the manufacturer's procedure.**
2. **Check the parking brake indicator light by turning the ignition key to the run position (do not start the engine) and observing the brake-warning lamp on the dash. Apply and release the parking brake.**
   a. **List your observations:**

> **NOTE** If the parking brake light did not go off, check the level of brake fluid in the master cylinder reservoir. If low, top up with the specified brake fluid. If it still is on, research the diagnostic procedure in the service information.

4. **Apply the parking brake. Ensure that no people, tools, or equipment are in front of or behind the vehicle. With instructor permission, start the vehicle and verify that the parking brake properly holds the vehicle when placed in drive and reverse.**

> **NOTE** Use extreme caution when performing this test. If the vehicle moves, stop.

   a. **Does the parking brake hold the vehicle? Yes: ________ No: ________**

5. **Determine necessary action(s):**

6. **Have your supervisor/instructor verify satisfactory completion of this procedure, any observations found, and any necessary action(s) recommended.**

Performance Rating

CDX Tasksheet Number: C633

☐	☐	☐	☐	☐
0	1	2	3	4

Supervisor/instructor signature ________________ Date ________

▶ TASK Check parking brake system and components for wear, binding, and corrosion; clean, lubricate, adjust, and/or replace as needed.

MAST 5F3

Time off________

Time on________

Total time________

CDX Tasksheet Number: C811

1. **Research the following specifications for this vehicle in the appropriate service information.**
   a. **Specified parking brake cable lubricant:** ________
   b. **Parking brake adjustment:** ________

2. **Safely raise and support the vehicle on the hoist. Trace all parking brake cables to each wheel's brake assembly. Inspect the cables for the following defects and list the location and cause of the defect(s):**
   a. **Wear:** ________
   b. **Rusting:** ________
   c. **Binding:** ________
   d. **Corrosion:** ________

3. **Clean, lubricate, or replace cables as necessary and list the actions performed:**

4. **Check the parking brake adjustment (this could be counting clicks of the ratchet assembly). List your observations:**

5. **If the parking brake needs adjustment, perform that now.**

6. **Have your supervisor/instructor verify satisfactory completion of this procedure, any observations found, and any necessary action(s) recommended.**

Performance Rating

CDX Tasksheet Number: C811

0	1	2	3	4
☐	☐	☐	☐	☐

Supervisor/instructor signature ________ Date ________

▶ TASK Check operation of brake stop light system.

MAST 5F5

Time off________

Time on________

Total time________

CDX Tasksheet Number: C272

1. **Research the correct brake light bulb number(s) in the appropriate service information.**
    a. **Specified brake lamp bulb number:** ____________________
    b. **High-mounted stop light bulb number, if equipped with replaceable bulbs:** ____________________

2. **Have another student step on the brake pedal while you observe the reaction of the brake lights (including the high-mounted stop light, if equipped). List your observation(s):**

3. **If the brake lights do not work properly, check simple things like individual bulbs to see if individual lights are out. If all of the brake lights are out, check the brake circuit fuse. List your findings:**

4. **Determine any necessary action(s):**

5. **Have your supervisor/instructor verify satisfactory completion of this procedure, any observations found, and any necessary action(s) recommended.**

Performance Rating

CDX Tasksheet Number: C272

☐	☐	☐	☐	☐
0	1	2	3	4

Supervisor/instructor signature ____________________ Date ____________

▶ TASK Diagnose wheel bearing noises, wheel shimmy, and vibration concerns; determine needed action.

MAST 5F1

Time off________

Time on________

Total time________

CDX Tasksheet Number: C267

Vehicle used for this activity:

Year ________ Make ________ Model ________

Odometer ________ VIN ________

1. **List the customer concern/complaint regarding a wheel bearing issue:**

2. **Research possible causes of the concern in the appropriate service information. List possible causes:**

3. **Follow the specified procedure for determining the cause of the complaint/concern. Depending on the actual fault, this could require many steps. List the steps you took to determine the fault:**

4. **List the cause of the concern/complaint:**

5. **List the necessary action(s) to correct this fault:**

6. **Have your supervisor/instructor verify satisfactory completion of this procedure, any observations found, and any necessary action(s) recommended.**

Performance Rating

CDX Tasksheet Number: C267

0	1	2	3	4

Supervisor/instructor signature _______________ Date _______

▶ TASK Remove, clean, inspect, repack, and install wheel bearings; replace seals; install hub and adjust bearings.

MAST 5F2

Time off________

Time on________

Total time________

CDX Tasksheet Number: C810

1. **Research the wheel bearing disassembly, cleaning, inspection, repacking, and installation procedure in the appropriate service information and list the following specifications:**
   a. **Specified wheel bearing grease:** ________________
   b. **Steps for adjusting the wheel bearing:**

   c. **Spindle nut final torque, if specified:** ________ **in-lb:** ________ **ft-lb:** ________ **N·m:** ________

2. **Remove the wheel bearings from one wheel assembly, following the specified procedure. Be sure to use the appropriate brake dust removal system to properly remove and dispose of any brake dust. Clean and inspect the wheel bearings and race. Also clean and inspect the spindle. List your observations:**

3. **Show your supervisor/instructor the wheel bearings and races. Supervisor's/instructor's initials:** ________________

> **NOTE** It may make sense to perform the next task, C273 at this time. Ask your instructor.

4. **Repack the wheel bearings with the proper grease. Install the inner bearing in the race and replace the old grease seal with a new one (being careful to not damage it).**

5. **Reinstall the hub and outer bearing onto the spindle.**

6. **Adjust the wheel bearing preload, or torque spindle nut (depending on application), according to the specified procedure.**

> **NOTE** Most adjustable wheel bearings require a fairly heavy torque to seat the bearings (example: 25 ft-lb) and a lighter torque to preload the bearing (example: 20 in-lb). Failure to loosen the bearing and preload it to the lower torque will result in burned-up bearings.

7. **Have your instructor verify the wheel bearing adjustment. Supervisor's/instructor's initials:** ________________

8. **Install a new cotter pin or secure the spindle nut, according to the specified procedure.**

9. **Have your supervisor/instructor verify satisfactory completion of this procedure, any observations found, and any necessary action(s) recommended.**

Performance Rating

CDX Tasksheet Number: C810

☐	☐	☐	☐	☐
0	1	2	3	4

Supervisor/instructor signature ____________________ Date ________

▶ TASK Replace wheel bearing and race.

MAST 5F6

Time off________

Time on________

Total time________

CDX Tasksheet Number: C273

1. **Research the wheel bearing and race disassembly and installation procedure in the appropriate service information and list the following specifications:**
   a. **Specified wheel bearing grease:** ________
   b. **Steps for adjusting the wheel bearing:**

   c. **Spindle nut final torque, if specified:** ________ **ft-lb/ N·m**

2. **Using a hammer and soft punch, carefully drive the race from the hub. Avoid scarring the surface of the hub with the punch and hammer.**

3. **Clean and inspect the wheel bearings and race. List your observations:**

4. **Show your supervisor/instructor the wheel bearing and race. Supervisor's/ instructor's initials:** ________

5. **Unless your supervisor/instructor directs you otherwise, replace the wheel bearing and race with new ones, following the specified procedure. Make sure the race is fully seated in the hub.**

6. **Repack the wheel bearings with the proper grease. Install the inner bearing in the race and replace the old grease seal with a new one.**

7. **Reinstall the hub and outer bearing onto the spindle.**

8. **Install the thrust washer and adjustment nut on the spindle. Adjust the wheel bearing preload, or torque spindle nut (depending on application), according to the specified procedure. Supervisor's/instructor's initials:** ________

9. **Install a new cotter pin, or secure the spindle nut, according to the specified procedure.**

10. **Have your supervisor/instructor verify satisfactory completion of this procedure, any observations found, and any necessary action(s) recommended.**

Performance Rating

CDX Tasksheet Number: C273

0	1	2	3	4
☐	☐	☐	☐	☐

Supervisor/instructor signature ______________________ Date ____________

▶ TASK Remove, reinstall, and/or replace sealed wheel bearing assembly.

MAST 5F7

CDX Tasksheet Number: C275

Time off__________

Time on__________

Total time__________

1. **Research the sealed wheel bearing assembly removal and installation procedure in the appropriate service information.**
    a. **Hub bolt torque: ________________ ft/lbs or N·m**
    b. **Axle nut torque (if equipped): ________________ ft/lbs or N·m**
2. **Remove the sealed wheel bearing assembly from the vehicle, following the specified procedure.**
3. **Show your supervisor/instructor the wheel bearing assembly. Supervisor's/instructor's initials: ________________**
4. **Replace or reinstall the wheel bearing assembly, again following the specified procedure. Be sure to properly torque all fasteners and replace any removed cotter pins with new cotter pins.**
5. **Have your supervisor/instructor verify satisfactory completion of this procedure, any observations found, and any necessary action(s) recommended.**

Performance Rating

CDX Tasksheet Number: C275

☐	☐	☐	☐	☐
0	1	2	3	4

Supervisor/instructor signature ________________________ Date __________

▶ TASK Inspect, remove, and/or replace bearings, hubs, and seals.

MAST 3D3

Time off________

Time on________

Total time________

CDX Tasksheet Number: C134

1. **Research the procedure and specifications for removing and replacing the FWD wheel bearing, hub, and seals in the appropriate service information.**
   a. **List any special tools required to perform this task:**

   b. **List any specific precautions when performing this task:**

   c. **List or print off and attach to this sheet the procedure for replacing the wheel bearing, seal, and hub:**

2. **If not already done, safely raise and support the vehicle on a hoist and remove the wheel bearing following the specified procedure.**

3. **Inspect the bearing, shaft, and hub for damage or wear. List your observations:**

4. **Determine any necessary action(s):**

5. **Have your supervisor/instructor verify removal and your observations. Supervisor's/instructor's initials: ________________**

6. **Following the specified procedure, replace the wheel bearing, seal, and hub. Make sure the bearing is fully seated and retained in the hub. List your observations:**

> **NOTE** Be sure to tighten all fasteners to the proper torque.

7. **Have your supervisor/instructor verify satisfactory completion of this procedure, any observations found, and any necessary action(s) recommended.**

Performance Rating

CDX Tasksheet Number: C134

0	1	2	3	4
☐	☐	☐	☐	☐

Supervisor/instructor signature ______________________ Date ________

▶ TASK Bleed the electronic brake control system hydraulic circuits.

MAST 5G6

Time off________

Time on________

Total time________

CDX Tasksheet Number: C637

1. **Research the correct procedure to bleed the system in the appropriate service information. List the steps here:**

2. **Using the identified procedure and equipment, bleed the electronic brake control system hydraulic circuits.**

3. **Determine any necessary action(s):**

4. **Have your supervisor/instructor verify satisfactory completion of this procedure, any observations found, and any necessary action(s) recommended.**

Performance Rating

CDX Tasksheet Number: C637

0	1	2	3	4
☐	☐	☐	☐	☐

Supervisor/instructor signature ________________ Date ________

▶ TASK Depressurize high-pressure components of an electronic brake control system.

MAST 5G5

Time off________

Time on________

Total time________

CDX Tasksheet Number: C812

1. **Research the procedure to depressurize the high-pressure components of the ABS system in the appropriate service information. List the steps to perform this task:**

2. **Perform the steps necessary to depressurize the ABS system, being careful to follow the specified procedure. Determine any necessary action(s):**

3. **Have your supervisor/instructor verify satisfactory completion of this procedure, any observations found, and any necessary action(s) recommended.**

Performance Rating

CDX Tasksheet Number: C812

0	1	2	3	4

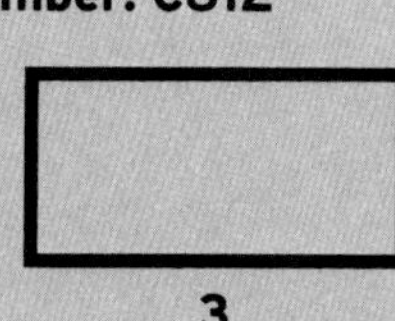

Supervisor/instructor signature ________________________________ Date ____________

▶ TASK Diagnose poor stopping, wheel lock-up, abnormal pedal feel, unwanted application, and noise concerns associated with the electronic brake control system; determine needed action.

MAST 5G3

Time off________

Time on________

Total time________

CDX Tasksheet Number: C635

1. **List the ABS brake-related customer complaint/concern:**

2. **Research the particular concern in the appropriate service information. List the possible causes:**

3. **Test the vehicle and diagnose poor stopping, wheel lock-up, abnormal pedal feel, unwanted application, and noise concerns associated with the electronic brake control system. List your tests and the results:**

4. **List the cause of the concern:**

5. **Determine any necessary action(s) to correct the fault:**

6. **Have your supervisor/instructor verify satisfactory completion of this procedure, any observations found, and any necessary action(s) recommended.**

Performance Rating

CDX Tasksheet Number: C635

☐	☐	☐	☐	☐
0	1	2	3	4

Supervisor/instructor signature ________________ Date ________

▶ TASK Diagnose electronic brake control system electronic control(s) and components by retrieving diagnostic trouble codes, and/or using recommended test equipment; determine needed action.

MAST 5G4

Time off______

Time on______

Total time______

CDX Tasksheet Number: C636

1. **List the ABS brake-related customer complaint/concern:**

2. **Research the particular concern in the appropriate service information. List the possible causes:**

3. **Use a scan tool to retrieve diagnostic trouble codes. List any codes and their descriptions:**

4. **Diagnose the electronic brake control system electronic control/s and the system components. List your tests and the results:**

5. **List the cause of the concern:**

6. **Determine any necessary action(s) to correct the fault:**

7. **Have your supervisor/instructor verify satisfactory completion of this procedure, any observations found, and any necessary action(s) recommended.**

Performance Rating

CDX Tasksheet Number: C636

0	1	2	3	4
☐	☐	☐	☐	☐

Supervisor/instructor signature ______________________ Date ________

▶ TASK Identify and inspect electronic brake control system components (ABS, TCS, ESC); determine needed action.

MAST 5G1

Time off________

Time on________

Total time________

CDX Tasksheet Number: C634

1. **Research the electronic brake control system description, theory of operation, and testing procedures for this vehicle in the appropriate service information.**
   a. **List the main components in the electronic brake control system:**

   b. **List the type of wheel speed sensor used:** ________________
   c. **Wheel speed sensor resistance (if inductive style):** ________ **ohms**

2. **Inspect the wheel speed sensors for integrity and condition.**
   a. **Wheel speed sensor resistance: (if inductive style)**
      Left front: ________ **ohms**
      Right front: ________ **ohms**
      Left rear: ________ **ohms**
      Right rear: ________ **ohms**
   b. **Wheel speed sensor lab scope pattern: Sketch the lab scope pattern of one wheel speed sensor while the wheel is turning.**

3. **Do the wheel speed sensors meet specifications? Yes:** ________ **No:** ________

4. **Have your supervisor/instructor verify satisfactory completion of this procedure, any observations found, and any necessary action(s) recommended.**

Performance Rating

CDX Tasksheet Number: C634

0	1	2	3	4

Supervisor/instructor signature ________________ Date ________

TASK Test, diagnose, and service electronic brake control system speed sensors (digital and analog), toothed ring (tone wheel), and circuits using a graphing multimeter (GMM)/digital storage oscilloscope (DSO) (includes output signal, resistance, shorts to voltage/ground, and frequency data). **MAST 5G7**

Time off________

Time on________

Total time________

CDX Tasksheet Number: C639

1. **List the ABS brake-related customer complaint/concern:**

2. **Research the particular concern in the appropriate service information. List the possible causes:**

3. **Carry out the tests using a graphing multimeter (GMM) or digital storage oscilloscope (DSO) and list your results. The tests should include:**
    a. **Output signal:** ________________
    b. **Resistance:** ________________
    c. **Shorts to voltage/ground:** ________________
    d. **Frequency data:** ________________

4. **Note your conclusions here:**

5. **Determine any necessary action(s) to correct the fault:**

6. **Have your supervisor/instructor verify satisfactory completion of this procedure, any observations found, and any necessary action(s) recommended.**

Performance Rating

CDX Tasksheet Number: C639

0	1	2	3	4
☐	☐	☐	☐	☐

Supervisor/instructor signature ________________ Date ________

▶ TASK Diagnose electronic brake control system braking concerns caused by vehicle modifications (tire size, curb height, final drive ratio, etc.). **MAST 5G8**

Time off________

Time on________

Total time________

CDX Tasksheet Number: C813

1. **List the ABS brake-related customer complaint/concern (caused by vehicle modifications):**

2. **Research the particular concern in the appropriate service information. List the possible cause(s):**

3. **Following the specified procedure, diagnose the electronic brake control concern (caused by vehicle modifications). List your tests and the results:**

4. **List the root cause of the problem:**

5. **Determine any necessary action(s) to correct the fault:**

6. **Have your supervisor/instructor verify satisfactory completion of this procedure, any observations found, and any necessary action(s) recommended.**

Performance Rating

CDX Tasksheet Number: C813

☐	☐	☐	☐	☐
0	1	2	3	4

Supervisor/instructor signature ________ Date ________

▶ TASK Research vehicle service information including fluid type, vehicle service history, service precautions, and technical service bulletins.

MAST 3A2

Time off________

Time on________

Total time________

CDX Tasksheet Number: C102

1. **Using the vehicle VIN for identification, use the appropriate source to access the vehicle's service history in relation to prior related drive train system work or customer concerns.**
   a. **List any related repairs/concerns, and their dates:**

2. **List the specified type of transmission fluid for this vehicle:** ____________

3. **Using the vehicle VIN for identification, access any relevant technical service bulletins for the particular vehicle you are working on in relation to any drive train system updates, precautions, or other service issues. List any related service bulletins:**

4. **Have your supervisor/instructor verify satisfactory completion of this procedure, any observations found, and any necessary action(s) recommended.**

Performance Rating

CDX Tasksheet Number: C102

0	1	2	3	4
☐	☐	☐	☐	☐

Supervisor/instructor signature ____________ Date ________

▶ TASK Identify and interpret drive train concerns; determine needed action.

Time off________

Time on________

Total time________

CDX Tasksheet Number: C101

1. **List the customer's transmission-related concern(s):**

2. **Research the particular concern in the appropriate service information. List the possible causes:**

3. **Inspect the vehicle to determine the cause of the concern. List the steps you took to determine the fault(s):**

4. **List the cause of the concern(s):**

5. **List the necessary action(s) to correct the fault(s):**

6. **Have your supervisor/instructor verify satisfactory completion of this procedure, any observations found, and any necessary action(s) recommended.**

Performance Rating

CDX Tasksheet Number: C101

☐	☐	☐	☐	☐
0	1	2	3	4

Supervisor/instructor signature ________________ Date ________

▶ TASK Demonstrate the use of the 3 Cs (concern, cause, and correction).

Additional Task

Time off________

Time on________

Total time________

CDX Tasksheet Number: N/A

1. **Using the following scenario, write up the 3 Cs as listed on most repair orders. Assume that the customer authorized the recommended repairs.**
   A late model half-ton pickup truck is brought to your shop with a manual transaxle concern. The customer tells you that the transmission started slipping a couple of days ago after his brother used it to haul several loads of gravel. You road test the vehicle and notice that it is slipping in all gears when under a moderate load. Also, the clutch pedal seems softer than normal, and there is a burning smell when you get back to the shop. You pull the vehicle onto a rack, and find the following:
   a. **The vehicle has 91,000 miles on it, but otherwise is in good condition.**
   b. **The transmission fluid is full and looks good.**
   c. **The slave cylinder is seeping brake fluid slightly from the dust boot, and the clutch master cylinder fluid level is a bit low.**
   d. **With the clutch inspection cover removed, there is a lot of clutch material and the burning smell is very strong.**
   e. **The rear shocks are leaking badly past the shaft seal.**

> NOTE Ask your instructor whether you should use a copy of the shop repair order or the 3 Cs below to record this information.

2. **Concern:**

3. **Cause:**

4. **Correction:**

5. **Other recommended service:**

6. **Have your supervisor/instructor verify satisfactory completion of this procedure, any observations found, and any necessary action(s) recommended.**

Performance Rating

CDX Tasksheet Number: N/A

☐	☐	☐	☐	☐
0	1	2	3	4

Supervisor/instructor signature _______________ Date _______

▶ TASK Inspect clutch pedal linkage, cables, automatic adjuster mechanisms, brackets, bushings, pivots, and springs; perform needed action.

MAST 3B2

Time off________

Time on________

Total time________

CDX Tasksheet Number: C107

1. **Research the procedure and specifications for inspecting and adjusting the clutch linkage in the appropriate service information.**
   a. **Clutch pedal height: ____________________ in/mm**
   b. **Clutch pedal free play: ____________________ in/mm**
   c. **Is this an adjustable clutch? Yes: __________ No: __________**
   d. **If yes, how is it adjusted?**

2. **Following the specified procedure, inspect the following parts for damage, wear, or missing components. List your observations for each.**
   a. **Clutch pedal linkage:**
   b. **Cable(s):**
   c. **Automatic adjuster mechanism, if equipped:**
   d. **Brackets:**
   e. **Bushings/guides/pivots:**

f. **Springs:**

3. **Measure the clutch pedal height: ______________________ in/mm**

4. **Measure the clutch pedal free play: ______________________ in/mm**

5. **Determine any necessary action(s):**

6. **Have your supervisor/instructor verify your answers.**
   Supervisor's/instructor's initials: ______________________

7. **Perform any necessary action(s) and list your observations:**

8. **Have your supervisor/instructor verify satisfactory completion of this procedure, any observations found, and any necessary action(s) recommended.**

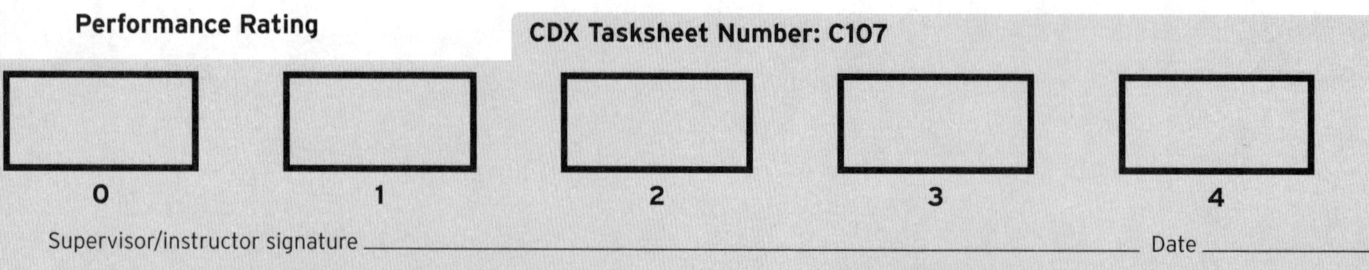

▶ TASK Check and adjust clutch master cylinder fluid level; check for leaks; use proper fluid type per manufacturer specification.

MAST 3B5

Time off________

Time on________

Total time________

CDX Tasksheet Number: C938

1. **Research the procedure and specifications for checking and adjusting the master cylinder fluid level in the appropriate service information.**
    a. **Specified clutch master cylinder fluid:** ____________________
    b. **Specified clutch master cylinder fluid replacement interval:** ____________________ **mi/km/mo**

2. **Check the clutch master cylinder fluid level and condition. List your observations:**

3. **Inspect the following clutch hydraulic system components for leaks. List your observations:**
    a. **Clutch master cylinder:**
    b. **Clutch slave cylinder (look under the dust boot):**
    c. **Hydraulic clutch lines and hoses:**

4. **Have your supervisor/instructor verify satisfactory completion of this procedure, any observations found, and any necessary action(s) recommended.**

Performance Rating

CDX Tasksheet Number: C938

0	1	2	3	4
☐	☐	☐	☐	☐

Supervisor/instructor signature ____________________ Date ________

▶ TASK Bleed clutch hydraulic system.

MAST 3B4

Time off________

Time on________

Total time________

CDX Tasksheet Number: C111

Vehicle used for this activity:

Year ____________ Make ________________________ Model________________________

Odometer____________________ VIN____

1. **Research the procedure and specifications for bleeding the clutch hydraulic system in the appropriate service information.**
    a. **Specified fluid:** ____
    b. **List or print off and attach to this sheet the steps to bleed the system:**

    c. **List any special tools needed for this task:**

2. **Following the specified procedure, inspect the following parts for damage, wear, or missing components. List your observations for each.**
    a. **Clutch master cylinder:**

    b. **Clutch slave cylinder:**

    c. **Lines (steel or plastic):**

d. Hoses (flexible):

3. Following the specified procedure, bleed the hydraulic clutch system, being careful not to run the reservoir low. List your observation(s):

4. Have your supervisor/instructor verify satisfactory completion of this procedure, any observations found, and any necessary action(s) recommended.

Performance Rating

CDX Tasksheet Number: C111

☐	☐	☐	☐	☐
0	1	2	3	4

Supervisor/instructor signature _______________ Date _______

▶ TASK Diagnose clutch noise, binding, slippage, pulsation, and chatter; determine needed action.

MAST 3B1

Time off________

Time on________

Total time________

CDX Tasksheet Number: C106

1. **List the customer concern(s) related to the conditions listed above:**

2. **If your instructor approves, test-drive the vehicle to verify the concern. List your observation(s):**

> **NOTE** If the clutch is spongy, you may need to do some preliminary checks such as checking the level of fluid in the hydraulic clutch master cylinder before test-driving the vehicle.

3. **Research the concern in the appropriate service information. List or print off and attach to this sheet the possible causes:**

   a. **List or print off and attach to this sheet the steps to diagnose this concern:**

4. **Following the specified procedure, diagnose the cause of the customer concern. List your steps and the results obtained:**

5. **Determine any necessary action(s) to correct the fault:**

6. **Have your supervisor/instructor verify satisfactory completion of this procedure, any observations found, and any necessary action(s) recommended.**

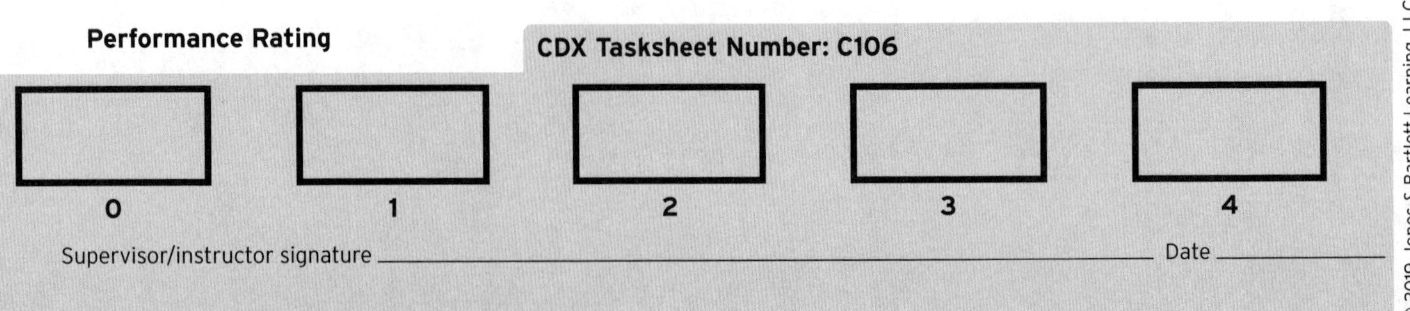
Performance Rating

CDX Tasksheet Number: C106

0 1 2 3 4

Supervisor/instructor signature ______________________ Date __________

▶ TASK Inspect flywheel and ring gear for wear, cracks, and discoloration; determine needed action.

MAST 3B6

Time off______

Time on______

Total time______

CDX Tasksheet Number: C847

1. **Research the procedure for inspecting the flywheel and ring gear in the appropriate service information. List any specifications or specific instructions for inspection:**

2. **Inspect the flywheel for wear, cracks, and discoloration. List your observations:**

3. **Inspect the ring gear for wear, chipped teeth, and cracks. List your observations:**

> NOTE It is common for the ring gear teeth to be worn in a pattern. For example, a four-cylinder engine will have greater wear every 180°, a six-cylinder engine every 120°, and an eight-cylinder engine every 90°. Therefore, be sure to inspect all of the teeth, not just a few of them.

4. **Determine any necessary action(s):**

5. **Have your supervisor/instructor verify satisfactory completion of this procedure, any observations found, and any necessary action(s) recommended.**

Performance Rating

CDX Tasksheet Number: C847

0	1	2	3	4
☐	☐	☐	☐	☐

Supervisor/instructor signature ______ Date ______

▶ TASK Measure flywheel runout and crankshaft end play; determine needed action.

MAST 3B7

Time off________

Time on________

Total time________

CDX Tasksheet Number: C848

1. **Research the specifications and procedure for measuring flywheel runout and crankshaft end play in the appropriate service information.**
   a. **Flywheel runout:** ________________ **in/mm**
   b. **Crankshaft end play:** ________________ **in/mm**
2. **If not already completed, following the specified procedure, remove the transmission/transaxle. List any observations:**
3. **Following the specified procedure, remove the pressure plate and clutch disc.**

> **NOTE** It is good practice to remove the pressure plate bolts evenly. This requires backing each bolt out a turn or two at a time to avoid warping the pressure plate. Also, have an assistant hold the pressure plate and clutch disc when they get close to becoming loose to avoid dropping them on the floor and damaging them or injuring your feet.

4. **Clean up any debris using an approved method for disposing of hazardous dust.**
5. **Following the specified procedure, measure the following.**
   a. **Flywheel runout:** ________________ **in/mm**
   b. **Crankshaft end play:** ________________ **in/mm**
6. **Determine any necessary action(s):**
7. **Have your supervisor/instructor verify satisfactory completion of this procedure, any observations found, and any necessary action(s) recommended.**

Performance Rating

CDX Tasksheet Number: C848

☐	☐	☐	☐	☐
0	1	2	3	4

Supervisor/instructor signature ________________ Date ________

▶ TASK Inspect and/or replace clutch pressure plate assembly, clutch disc, release (throw-out) bearing, linkage, and pilot bearing/bushing (as applicable).

MAST 3B3

Time off________

Time on________

Total time________

CDX Tasksheet Number: C608

1. **Research the procedure and any specifications for inspecting the clutch assembly.**
    a. **List any specifications or specific instructions for inspection:**

    b. **Flywheel-to-crankshaft bolt torque:** ________________ **ft-lb/N·m**
        i. **Threadlock required: Yes:** ________ **No:** ________
    c. **Pressure plate-to-flywheel bolt torque:** ________________ **ft-lb/N·m**
    d. **Pilot bushing/bearing lubricant, if applicable:** ________________

2. **Inspect each of the following and list your observations.**
    a. **Pressure plate assembly:**

    b. **Clutch disc:**

    c. **Release (throw-out) bearing and linkage:**

    d. **Pilot bearing/bushing:**

3. **Determine any necessary action(s):**

4. **Have your supervisor/instructor verify your observations and recommendations and initial below.**
   a. **Supervisor's/instructor's initials:** ______________________

5. **With your instructor's permission, replace any worn parts with new/remanufactured components.**

6. **Following the specified procedure, install the pilot bushing/bearing, if removed. Lubricate it with the specified lubricant, if applicable.**

7. **Following the specified procedure, install the flywheel. Be sure to torque the flywheel bolts.**

8. **Following the specified procedure, install the clutch disc and pressure plate. Use an appropriate clutch alignment tool to ensure proper positioning of the clutch disc.**

> NOTE The pressure plate bolts should be tightened down evenly. This is usually done by tightening each bolt a turn or two, one at a time, until the pressure plate is evenly seated on the flywheel surface. Then, torque each bolt according to the specified torque and sequence.

9. **Install the release (throw-out) bearing and linkage.**

10. **List any observation(s):**

11. **Have your supervisor/instructor verify satisfactory completion of this procedure, any observations found, and any necessary action(s) recommended.**

Performance Rating | **CDX Tasksheet Number: C608**

☐	☐	☐	☐	☐
0	1	2	3	4

Supervisor/instructor signature ______________________ Date ____________

▶ TASK Describe the operational characteristics of an electronically controlled manual transmission/transaxle.

MAST 3C2

Time off________

Time on________

Total time________

CDX Tasksheet Number: C611

Vehicle used for this activity:

Year ________ Make ________________ Model________________

Odometer____________ VIN________________________

1. **Research the description and operation of an electronically controlled manual transmission/transaxle in the appropriate service information.**
   a. **How many forward speeds does this transmission have?**

   b. **How do the electronics interface with the transmission to control the transmission?**

   c. **How does this transmission achieve neutral?**

   d. **What type of fluid does this transmission use?** ________________
   e. **What is the fluid capacity?** ________________ **qt/lt**
   f. **What type of clutch(es) does this transmission use?**

2. **Have your supervisor/instructor verify satisfactory completion of this procedure, any observations found, and any necessary action(s) recommended.**

Performance Rating

CDX Tasksheet Number: C611

0	1	2	3	4
☐	☐	☐	☐	☐

Supervisor/instructor signature ________________________ Date ________

▶ TASK Check fluid condition; check for leaks; determine needed action. **MAST 3A3**

Time off________

Time on________

Total time________

CDX Tasksheet Number: C691

1. **List the transmission designation for this vehicle:** ____________________

2. **Research the following specifications for this vehicle in the appropriate service information.**

   a. **Fluid type:** ____________________
   b. **Fluid capacity:** ____________________ **qt/lt**
   c. **How is the fluid level checked?**

3. **Safely raise and secure the vehicle on a hoist.**

4. **Following the specified procedure, check the fluid level and list your observation(s):**

5. **Inspect the condition of the fluid. Look for contaminants, metal shavings, and degraded fluid condition. List your observation(s):**

6. **Inspect the transmission/transaxle assembly for leaks.**

   a. **Identify and list the source of any leak(s):**

7. **Determine any necessary action(s):**

8. **Have your supervisor/instructor verify satisfactory completion of this procedure, any observations found, and any necessary action(s) recommended.**

Performance Rating

CDX Tasksheet Number: C691

☐	☐	☐	☐	☐
0	1	2	3	4

Supervisor/instructor signature ____________________ Date ________

▶ TASK Drain and refill manual transmission/transaxle and final drive unit; use proper fluid type per manufacturer specification.

MAST 3A4

Time off________

Time on________

Total time________

CDX Tasksheet Number: C105

1. **Research the following specifications and procedure in the appropriate service information.**
   a. **Transmission/transaxle service interval: ________________ km/mi**
   b. **Transmission/transaxle fluid type: ________________**
   c. **Transmission/transaxle fluid capacity: ________________ qt/lt**
   d. **Final drive service interval: ________________ km/mi**
   e. **Final drive fluid type: ________________**
   f. **Final drive fluid capacity: ________________ qt/lt**
2. **Following the specified procedure, drain the transmission/transaxle fluid into a clean drain pan. Inspect any residue and debris in the bottom of the drain pan. List your observations:**
3. **Determine any necessary action(s):**
4. **Drain the final drive unit (if separate from the transmission) into a clean drain pan. Inspect any residue and debris in the bottom of the drain pan. List your observations:**
5. **Have your supervisor/instructor verify fluid removal and your answers. Supervisor's/instructor's initials: ________________**
6. **Following the specified procedure, refill the transmission/transaxle and final drive unit. Replace all fill plugs and tighten them to the proper torque. List your observations:**
7. **Have your supervisor/instructor verify satisfactory completion of this procedure, any observations found, and any necessary action(s) recommended.**

Performance Rating

CDX Tasksheet Number: C105

☐	☐	☐	☐	☐
0	**1**	**2**	**3**	**4**

Supervisor/instructor signature ________________ Date ________

▶ TASK Diagnose noise concerns through the application of transmission/transaxle powerflow principles.

Time off________

Time on________

Total time________

CDX Tasksheet Number: C609

1. **List the transmission/transaxle noise-related customer concern:**

2. **Research the concern in the appropriate service information and list the possible causes:**

3. **Following the specified procedure, use powerflow flowcharts to identify the cause of the noise concern. List your tests and observations:**

4. **List the cause of the noise concern:**

5. **Determine any necessary action(s) to correct the fault:**

6. **Have your supervisor/instructor verify satisfactory completion of this procedure, any observations found, and any necessary action(s) recommended.**

Performance Rating

CDX Tasksheet Number: C609

0	1	2	3	4

Supervisor/instructor signature ________________ Date ________

▶ TASK Diagnose hard shifting and jumping out of gear concerns; determine needed action.

MAST 3C4

Time off________

Time on________

Total time________

CDX Tasksheet Number: C693

Vehicle used for this activity:

Year ________ Make ______________ Model______________

Odometer____________ VIN________________________

1. **List the hard shifting or jumping out of gear customer concern:**

2. **Research the concern in the appropriate service information and list the possible causes:**

3. **Following the specified procedure, diagnose the fault. List your tests and observations:**

4. **List the cause of the hard shifting or jumping out of gear concern:**

5. **Determine any necessary action(s) to correct the fault:**

6. **Have your supervisor/instructor verify satisfactory completion of this procedure, any observations found, and any necessary action(s) recommended.**

Performance Rating

CDX Tasksheet Number: C693

☐	☐	☐	☐	☐
0	1	2	3	4

Supervisor/instructor signature ____________________ Date ________

▶ TASK Diagnose transaxle final drive assembly noise and vibration concerns; determine needed action.

MAST 3C5

Time off________

Time on________

Total time________

CDX Tasksheet Number: C887

Vehicle used for this activity:

Year ____________ Make ________________________ Model ________________________

Odometer ____________________ VIN ____

1. **List the final drive noise or vibration customer concern:**

2. **Research the concern in the appropriate service information and list the possible causes:**

3. **Following the specified procedure, diagnose the fault. List your tests and observations:**

4. **List the cause of the noise or vibration concern:**

5. **Determine any necessary action(s) to correct the fault:**

6. **Have your supervisor/instructor verify satisfactory completion of this procedure, any observations found, and any necessary action(s) recommended.**

Performance Rating **CDX Tasksheet Number: C887**

☐	☐	☐	☐	☐
0	1	2	3	4

Supervisor/instructor signature ________________________________ Date ____________

▶ TASK Disassemble, clean, and reassemble transmission/transaxle components.

MAST 3C6

Time off________

Time on________

Total time________

CDX Tasksheet Number: C910

1. **Research the procedure to disassemble, clean, and reassemble the transmission/transaxle in the appropriate service information.**
   a. **List any special tools required for this task:**

   b. **List, or print off and attach to this sheet, the procedure to disassemble and reassemble the transmission/transaxle:**

2. **Following the specified procedure, disassemble the transmission/transaxle, ensuring that you note their location and orientation. Make notes or take pictures as appropriate. Lay them out in a logical manner to facilitate reassembly.**

> NOTE Round objects such as gears, shafts, ball bearings, roller bearings, and bushings can roll off of the work table if not secured, causing personal injury. This could also lead to damage or loss of the components. Always lay round objects on their side when possible, or store them in a work tray to prevent rolling.

3. **Clean the components according to the specified procedure. Make sure you relocate them in the same logical sequence as before.**

4. **Perform a preliminary visual inspection of the components. This is an initial inspection designed to identify major issues with the transmission/transaxle. Further inspection of the subunits and parts will occur as you perform the next several tasks.**
   List your observations:

5. **Have your supervisor/instructor verify the initial disassembly and your observations.**
   a. **Supervisor's/instructor's initials:** ________________ **Date:** ________________

▶ TASK Inspect, adjust, lubricate, and/or replace shift linkages, brackets, bushings, cables, pivots, and levers.

MAST 3C1

Time off________

Time on________

Total time________

CDX Tasksheet Number: C768

1. **Research the procedure and specifications for inspecting, adjusting, lubricating, and replacing shift linkages in the appropriate service information.**
   a. **List or print off and attach to this sheet the procedure for adjusting the shift linkages, if applicable:**

2. **Following the specified procedure, inspect and lubricate the shift linkage components. List your observations for each component.**
   a. **Shift linkages:**

   b. **Brackets:**

   c. **Bushings:**

   d. **Cables:**

e. Pivots:

f. Levers:

3. Following the specified procedure, replace and/or adjust each shift linkage. List your observations:

4. Have your supervisor/instructor verify satisfactory completion of this procedure, any observations found, and any necessary action(s) recommended.

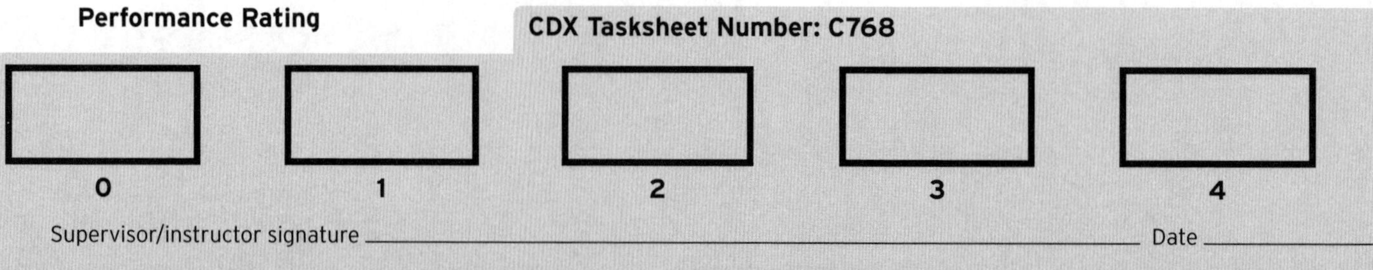

Performance Rating

CDX Tasksheet Number: C768

0 1 2 3 4

Supervisor/instructor signature _______________ Date _______

▶ TASK Check fluid condition; check for leaks; determine needed action.

MAST 3A3

Time off________

Time on________

Total time________

CDX Tasksheet Number: C691

1. **List the transmission designation for this vehicle:** ________________

2. **Research the following specifications for this vehicle in the appropriate service information.**
   a. **Fluid type:** ________________
   b. **Fluid capacity:** ________________ **qt/lt**
   c. **How is the fluid level checked?**

3. **Safely raise and secure the vehicle on a hoist.**

4. **Following the specified procedure, check the fluid level and list your observation(s):**

5. **Inspect the condition of the fluid. Look for contaminants, metal shavings, and degraded fluid condition. List your observation(s):**

6. **Inspect the transmission/transaxle assembly for leaks.**
   a. **Identify and list the source of any leak(s):**

7. **Determine any necessary action(s):**

8. **Have your supervisor/instructor verify satisfactory completion of this procedure, any observations found, and any necessary action(s) recommended.**

Performance Rating

CDX Tasksheet Number: C691

0	1	2	3	4

Supervisor/instructor signature ________________ Date ________

▶ TASK Check and adjust differential case fluid level; use proper fluid type per manufacturer specification.

Time off_______________

Time on_______________

Total time_______________

CDX Tasksheet Number: C911

1. **List the drive axle designation for this vehicle:** _______________
2. **Research the following specifications for this vehicle in the appropriate service information.**
    a. **Fluid type:** _______________
    b. **Fluid capacity:** _______________ **qt/lt**
    c. **How is the fluid level checked?**
    d. **Are any additives required? Yes:** _______ **No:** _______
        i. **If yes, what additive?** _______________
3. **Safely raise and secure the vehicle on a hoist.**
4. **Check the fluid level and adjust as necessary with the proper fluid. List your observation(s):**
5. **Inspect the drive axle assembly for leaks.**
    a. **Identify and list the source of any leak(s):**
6. **Inspect the condition of the fluid. Look for contaminants, metal shavings, and degraded fluid condition. List your observation(s):**
7. **Determine any necessary action(s):**
8. **Have your supervisor/instructor verify satisfactory completion of this procedure, any observations found, and any necessary action(s) recommended.**

Performance Rating

CDX Tasksheet Number: C911

0	1	2	3	4
☐	☐	☐	☐	☐

Supervisor/instructor signature _______________ Date _______________

▶ TASK Drain and refill differential case; use proper fluid type per manufacturer specification.

MAST
3E1:3

Time off__________

Time on__________

Total time__________

CDX Tasksheet Number: C912

Vehicle used for this activity:

Year __________ Make ____________________ Model____________________

Odometer________________ VIN____________________________________

1. **Research the following specifications for this vehicle in the appropriate service information.**
   a. **Fluid type:**__________________________________
   b. **Fluid capacity:** __________________ **qt/lt**
   c. **Differential fluid service interval:** __________________ **mi/km**
   d. **How is fluid drained from this differential housing?**

2. **Safely raise and secure the vehicle on a hoist.**

3. **Following the specified procedure, drain the fluid from the differential housing. List your observations:**

4. **Have your supervisor/instructor verify removal of the fluid, and your observations. Supervisor's/instructor's initials:** __________________

5. **Replace the drain plug or rear cover making sure the plug or bolts are tightened properly.**

6. **Fill the differential housing to the proper level with the specified lubricant.**

> NOTE Some differentials require special additives. Always check the service information to determine the proper fluid or additives.

7. **Have your supervisor/instructor verify satisfactory completion of this procedure, any observations found, and any necessary action(s) recommended.**

Performance Rating

CDX Tasksheet Number: C912

☐	☐	☐	☐	☐
0	**1**	**2**	**3**	**4**

Supervisor/instructor signature ____________________________________ Date ____________

▶ TASK Check shaft balance and phasing; measure shaft runout; measure and adjust driveline angles.

MAST 3D5

Time off________

Time on________

Total time________

CDX Tasksheet Number: C779

Vehicle used for this activity:

Year ________ Make ________ Model ________

Odometer ________ VIN ________

1. **Research the procedure and specifications for inspecting, measuring, and adjusting the driveline balance, phasing, and angles in the appropriate service information.**
    a. **List any special tools required to perform this task:**

    b. **List any specific precautions when performing this task:**

    c. **List any specifications for balance, phasing, runout, and driveline angles:**

    d. **List or print off and attach to this sheet the procedure for inspecting, measuring, and adjusting the driveline balance, phasing, and angles:**

2. **Safely raise and secure the vehicle on a hoist. Make sure the parking brake is released and the transmission is in neutral.**

3. Check the drive shaft for phasing. List your observation(s):

4. Measure drive shaft runout: ______________________ in/mm

5. Measure driveline angles.
   a. Front: ______________________ degrees
   b. Center (if specified): ______________________ degrees
   c. Rear: ______________________ degrees

6. Check the drive shaft for balance. List your observation(s):

7. Determine any necessary action(s):

8. Have your supervisor/instructor verify satisfactory completion of this procedure, any observations found, and any necessary action(s) recommended.

Performance Rating

CDX Tasksheet Number: C779

0	1	2	3	4
☐	☐	☐	☐	☐

Supervisor/instructor signature ______________________ Date ______________

▶ TASK Diagnose universal joint noise and vibration concerns; perform needed action.

MAST 3D2

Time off________

Time on________

Total time________

CDX Tasksheet Number: C133

Vehicle used for this activity:

Year ____________ Make ______________________ Model ______________________

Odometer __________________ VIN ______________________________________

1. **List the universal joint-related customer concern:**

2. **With your instructor's permission, test-drive the vehicle in an open area on a firm surface. Listen for a distinctive squeaking noise or clunking sound coming from under the vehicle, which is usually worse at low speeds. Universal joints can also cause a vibration at low speeds due to intermittent binding, or at higher speeds due to causing the drive shaft to be located off center. List your observations:**

3. **Safely raise and secure the vehicle on a hoist and inspect the universal joints for looseness, wear, and damage. List your observations:**

> **NOTE** Make sure the parking brake is not applied and the transmission is in neutral. This will allow you to turn the drive shaft to check it for play and binding in various positions.

4. **Determine any necessary action(s):**

5. **Have your supervisor/instructor verify your observations and diagnosis.**
   Supervisor's/instructor's initials: ____________________

6. Perform any necessary action(s) following the specified procedure. List your observations:

> **NOTE** Be sure to tighten all fasteners to the proper torque.

7. Have your supervisor/instructor verify satisfactory completion of this procedure, any observations found, and any necessary action(s) recommended.

Performance Rating

CDX Tasksheet Number: C133

☐	☐	☐	☐	☐
0	1	2	3	4

Supervisor/instructor signature ______________________ Date __________

▶ TASK Measure drive axle flange runout and shaft end play; determine needed action.

MAST 3E3:4

Time off________

Time on________

Total time________

CDX Tasksheet Number: C850

Vehicle used for this activity:

Year ________ Make ________ Model ________

Odometer ________ VIN ________

1. **Research the procedure and specifications for measuring the drive axle flange and shaft end play in the appropriate service information.**
   a. **Maximum specified axle flange runout: ________ in/mm**
   b. **Specified axle shaft end play: ________ in/mm**
2. **Perform an initial visual inspection of the axle flange. List your observation(s):**
3. **Following the specified procedure, measure the axle flange runout: ________ in/mm**
4. **Following the specified procedure, measure the axle shaft end play: ________ in/mm**
5. **Determine any necessary action(s):**
6. **Have your supervisor/instructor verify satisfactory completion of this procedure, any observations found, and any necessary action(s) recommended.**

Performance Rating

CDX Tasksheet Number: C850

0	1	2	3	4
☐	☐	☐	☐	☐

Supervisor/instructor signature ________ Date ________

▶ TASK Remove and replace drive axle shafts. **MAST 3E3:2**

Time off________

Time on________

Total time________

CDX Tasksheet Number: C155

Vehicle used for this activity:

Year ________ Make ________ Model ________

Odometer ________ VIN ________

1. **Research the procedure and specifications for replacing the drive axle shafts in the appropriate service information.**
   a. **Specified retainer bolt torque, if equipped: ________ ft-lb/N·m**
   b. **List or print off and attach to this sheet the steps to replace the axle shaft:**

2. **Following the specified procedure, remove the axle shaft. List your observation(s):**

3. **Have your supervisor/instructor verify removal and your observations. Supervisor's/instructor's initials: ________**

> **NOTE** You may want to skip ahead to the next task while the axle shaft is removed. Return here once that task is completed to reinstall the axle shaft.

4. **Following the specified procedure, reinstall the axle shaft. Be sure to tighten all fasteners to the specified torque. List your observation(s):**

5. **Have your supervisor/instructor verify satisfactory completion of this procedure, any observations found, and any necessary action(s) recommended.**

Performance Rating

CDX Tasksheet Number: C155

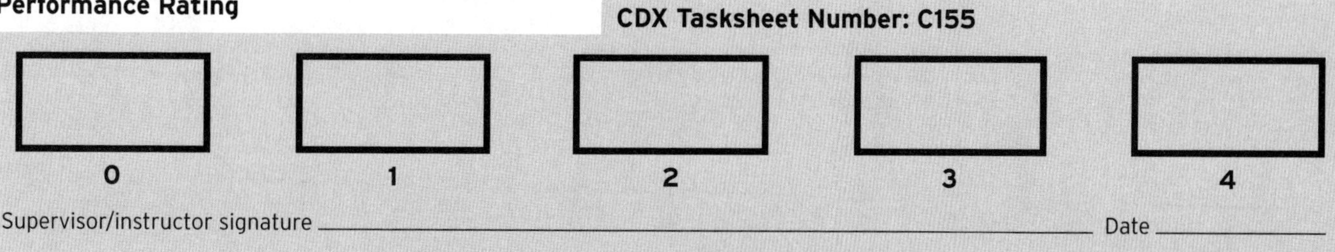

▶ TASK Inspect and replace drive axle shaft seals, bearings, and retainers.

MAST
3E3:3

Time off________

Time on________

Total time________

CDX Tasksheet Number: C156

Vehicle used for this activity:

Year ____________ Make ________________________ Model ________________________

Odometer ____________________ VIN ____

1. **Research the procedure and specifications for inspecting and replacing the seals, bearings, and retainers in the appropriate service information.**
    a. **List or print off and attach to this sheet the steps for performing this task:**

2. **Following the specified procedure, inspect each component and list your observations.**
    a. **Seal(s):**
    b. **Bearing(s):**
    c. **Retainer(s):**

3. **Remove the bearing(s), seal(s), and retainer(s). List your observations:**

4. **Have your supervisor/instructor verify removal and your observations. Supervisor's/instructor's initials:** ______________

5. **Reinstall the bearing(s), seal(s), and retainer(s). List your observations:**

6. **Have your supervisor/instructor verify satisfactory completion of this procedure, any observations found, and any necessary action(s) recommended.**

Performance Rating

CDX Tasksheet Number: C156

0	1	2	3	4

Supervisor/instructor signature ______________________ Date ________

▶ TASK Inspect, service, and/or replace shafts, yokes, boots, and universal/CV joints.

Time off________

Time on________

Total time________

CDX Tasksheet Number: C849

1. **Research the procedure and specifications to inspect, service, and replace shafts, yokes, boots, and universal/CV joints in the appropriate service information.**
    a. **List any special tools required to perform this task:**

    b. **List any specific precautions when performing this task:**

    c. **List or print off and attach to this sheet the procedure for servicing universal/CV joints, shafts, and boots:**

2. **If not already done, safely raise and support the vehicle on a hoist and inspect the half shafts and boots. List your observations:**

3. **Following the specified procedure, remove the worn half shaft(s).**
4. **With your instructor's permission, disassemble the half shaft(s) following the specified procedure.**
5. **Clean and inspect all parts. List your observations for each.**
    a. **Shaft(s):**

    b. **Yoke(s):**

c. **Boots (and clamps):**

d. **CV joint(s) (including any balls or rollers):**

6. **Determine any necessary action(s):**

7. **Have your supervisor/instructor verify disassembly and your observations. Supervisor's/instructor's initials: ___________________**

NOTE You may want to continue on with the next task once the half shaft(s) are reassembled and removed. If so, return here to complete this task once you are ready to reinstall the half shaft(s).

8. **Perform any necessary actions to service the half shaft(s) and reinstall them in the vehicle following the specified procedure. List your observations:**

NOTE Be sure to tighten all fasteners to the proper torque.

9. **Have your supervisor/instructor verify satisfactory completion of this procedure, any observations found, and any necessary action(s) recommended.**

Performance Rating

CDX Tasksheet Number: C849

0	1	2	3	4
☐	☐	☐	☐	☐

Supervisor/instructor signature ___________________ Date ___________

▶ TASK Inspect, remove, and/or replace bearings, hubs, and seals. **MAST 3D3**

Time off________

Time on________

Total time________

CDX Tasksheet Number: C134

1. **Research the procedure and specifications for removing and replacing the FWD wheel bearing, hub, and seals in the appropriate service information.**
   a. **List any special tools required to perform this task:**

   b. **List any specific precautions when performing this task:**

   c. **List or print off and attach to this sheet the procedure for replacing the wheel bearing, seal, and hub:**

2. **If not already done, safely raise and support the vehicle on a hoist and remove the wheel bearing following the specified procedure.**
3. **Inspect the bearing, shaft, and hub for damage or wear. List your observations:**

4. **Determine any necessary action(s):**

5. **Have your supervisor/instructor verify removal and your observations. Supervisor's/instructor's initials: ________________**

6. **Following the specified procedure, replace the wheel bearing, seal, and hub. Make sure the bearing is fully seated and retained in the hub. List your observations:**

> **NOTE** Be sure to tighten all fasteners to the proper torque.

7. **Have your supervisor/instructor verify satisfactory completion of this procedure, any observations found, and any necessary action(s) recommended.**

Performance Rating

CDX Tasksheet Number: C134

☐	☐	☐	☐	☐
0	1	2	3	4

Supervisor/instructor signature ______________________ Date ________

▶ TASK Diagnose noise and vibration concerns; determine needed action.

MAST 3E1:4

Time off________

Time on________

Total time________

CDX Tasksheet Number: C138

1. **List the drive axle noise and vibration-related customer concern:**

2. **Research the concern in the appropriate service information.**
   a. **List the possible causes of the concern:**
   b. **List, or print off and attach to this sheet, the specified procedure for diagnosing the concern:**

3. **Perform the appropriate tests, following the specified procedure. List your observation(s):**

4. **List the cause of the concern:**

5. **Determine any necessary action(s) to correct the fault:**

6. **Have your supervisor/instructor verify satisfactory completion of this procedure, any observations found, and any necessary action(s) recommended.**

Performance Rating

CDX Tasksheet Number: C138

0	1	2	3	4

Supervisor/instructor signature ________________ Date ________

▶ TASK Diagnose drive axle shafts, bearings, and seals for noise, vibration, and fluid leakage concerns; determine needed action.

MAST 3E3:5

Time off________

Time on________

Total time________

CDX Tasksheet Number: C153

1. **List the customer concern:**

2. **With your instructor's permission, test-drive the vehicle in an open area with minimal noise on a smooth road surface. Listen for excessive noise while gradually increasing speed. List your observation(s):**

> NOTE A worn wheel bearing will usually make noise in a manner proportional to speed. When you are traveling at a speed that is making the noise, it is good practice to put the vehicle in neutral and allow the vehicle to coast. If the wheel bearing(s) is (are) worn, this will cause no considerable difference in sound. Also, try different transmission gears to rule out transmission- and clutch-related noises.

3. **Safely raise and secure the vehicle on a hoist.**

4. **Perform a visual inspection for obvious damage or leaks, paying particular attention to the brake backing plates and center differential. List your observation(s):**

5. **With your instructor's permission, run the vehicle in gear on the hoist while listening to the wheel bearings with a stethoscope. Make sure the vehicle is very secure on the hoist. List your observation(s):**

6. **Determine any necessary action(s):**

7. **Have your supervisor/instructor verify satisfactory completion of this procedure, any observations found, and any necessary action(s) recommended.**

Performance Rating

CDX Tasksheet Number: C153

0	1	2	3	4
☐	☐	☐	☐	☐

Supervisor/instructor signature ____________________ Date __________

▶ TASK Inspect and replace drive axle shaft wheel studs.

MAST 3E3:1

Time off________

Time on________

Total time________

CDX Tasksheet Number: C154

Vehicle used for this activity:

Year ____________ Make ________________________ Model ________________________

Odometer ____________________ VIN ____

1. **Research the procedure and specifications for replacing the axle shaft wheel studs in the appropriate service information.**
   a. **There are generally two standard procedures for replacing wheel studs. One is to remove the hub from the vehicle and use a hydraulic press to remove and install the studs. The other is to use a hammer to drive out the old stud, and then use washers and the flat side of the lug nut to draw the new stud into the hub. Which method does the service information describe for this vehicle?**

   b. **List any special tools or procedures for this task:**

   c. **Lug nut torque: ______________ ft-lb/N·m**
2. **Safely raise and secure the vehicle on a hoist.**
3. **Remove the wheel assembly and inspect the lug nuts and wheel studs. List your observations and any necessary actions:**

4. **Have your supervisor/instructor verify your observations. Supervisor's/instructor's initials: ______________**
5. **Remove the damaged wheel stud(s) from the hub. Supervisor's/instructor's initials: ______________**
6. **Install the new wheel stud(s) in the hub, following all service information instructions.**

7. **Have your supervisor/instructor verify satisfactory completion of this procedure, any observations found, and any necessary action(s) recommended.**

Performance Rating

CDX Tasksheet Number: C154

0	1	2	3	4

Supervisor/instructor signature ____________ Date ______

▶ TASK Diagnose noise, slippage, and chatter concerns; determine needed action.

Time off________

Time on________

Total time________

CDX Tasksheet Number: C784

1. **List the limited slip differential customer concern:**

2. **Research the procedure and specifications to diagnose noise, slipping, and chatter concerns in the appropriate service information.**
   a. **List or print off and attach to this sheet the steps to diagnose this concern:**

   b. **List the specified lubricant and/or additive:** ________

3. **Following the specified procedure, diagnose the customer concern. List your tests and results:**

4. **List the cause(s) of the concern:**

5. **List the necessary action(s) to correct the concern:**

6. **Have your supervisor/instructor verify satisfactory completion of this procedure, any observations found, and any necessary action(s) recommended.**

Performance Rating

CDX Tasksheet Number: C784

☐	☐	☐	☐	☐
0	1	2	3	4

Supervisor/instructor signature ________ Date ________

▶ TASK Diagnose constant-velocity (CV) joint noise and vibration concerns; determine needed action.

MAST 3D1

Time off________

Time on________

Total time________

CDX Tasksheet Number: C132

1. **List the CV-related customer concern:**

2. **With your instructor's permission, test-drive the vehicle in an open area on a firm surface. Turn the steering wheel to its maximum lock position and drive smoothly in a tight circle. Listen for a distinctive clicking or knocking noise coming from one or more corners of the vehicle. List your observations:**

3. **Repeat step 2, turning the steering wheel in the other direction while driving in a tight circle. List your observations:**

4. **Safely raise and secure the vehicle on a hoist and visually inspect the CV joint boots for splits and tears, or signs of grease leakage from the boot or joint housing. List your observations:**

5. **Check for excessive play or binding in the inboard and outboard CV joints. List your observations:**

6. **Determine any necessary action(s):**

7. **Have your supervisor/instructor verify satisfactory completion of this procedure, any observations found, and any necessary action(s) recommended.**

Performance Rating

CDX Tasksheet Number: C132

0	1	2	3	4

Supervisor/instructor signature __________ Date __________

▶ TASK Inspect and replace companion flange and/or pinion seal; measure companion flange runout.

MAST 3E1:5

Time off________

Time on________

Total time________

CDX Tasksheet Number: C889

Vehicle used for this activity:

Year ________ Make ________ Model ________

Odometer ________ VIN ________

1. **Research the procedure and specifications for inspecting and replacing the companion flange and pinion seal in the appropriate service information.**
    a. **Maximum allowable companion flange runout (if specified): ________ in/mm**
    b. **Companion flange nut torque: ________ ft-lb/N·m**
    c. **Drive shaft-to-drive axle bolt torque: ________ ft-lb/N·m**
2. **Safely raise and secure the vehicle on a hoist.**
3. **Perform an initial visual inspection of the companion flange and pinion seal. List your observation(s):**
4. **Following the specified procedure, remove the drive shaft.**
5. **Measure the companion flange runout, if possible: ________ in/mm**
6. **Following the specified procedure, remove the companion flange and pinion seal. Inspect the following components for damage or wear.**
    a. **Companion flange:**
    b. **Pinion seal:**
    c. **Pinion shaft sealing surface:**

7. **Determine any necessary action(s):**

8. **Have your supervisor/instructor verify removal and your observations. Supervisor's/instructor's initials: ________________**

> **NOTE** If you are tasked with disassembling the drive axle assembly, continue on with the following tasks and return here when you are ready to reinstall the pinion seal and companion flange.

9. **Following the specified procedure, replace the pinion seal and companion flange. Be sure to properly tighten the companion flange nut. Once torqued, check the turning effort required to rotate the companion flange. List your observation(s):**

10. **Re-measure the companion flange runout: ________________ in/mm**

    a. **If the runout is not within specifications, inform your instructor.**

11. **Reinstall the drive shaft and any other removed components. Torque all fasteners to specifications.**

12. **Have your supervisor/instructor verify satisfactory completion of this procedure, any observations found, and any necessary action(s) recommended.**

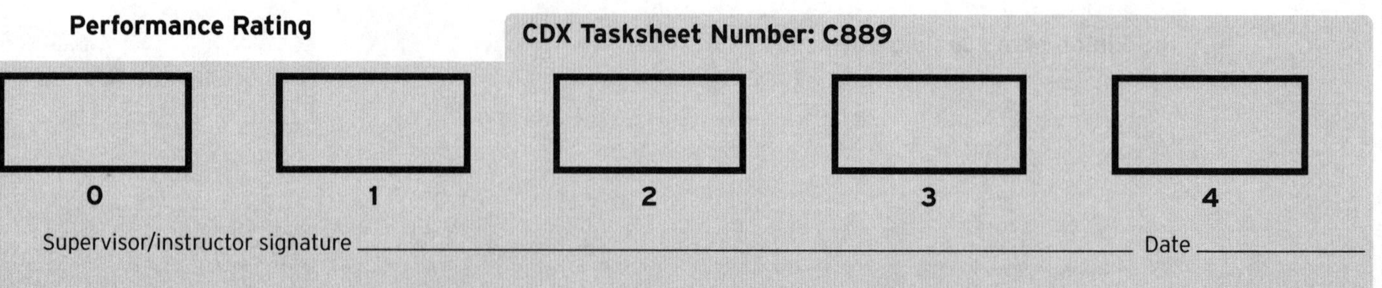
Performance Rating

CDX Tasksheet Number: C889

0 1 2 3 4

Supervisor/instructor signature ________________________________ Date ____________

▶ TASK Inspect ring gear and measure runout; determine needed action.

MAST 3E1:6

Time off________

Time on________

Total time________

CDX Tasksheet Number: C780

Vehicle used for this activity:

Year ____________ Make ______________________ Model ______________________

Odometer ______________________ VIN ______________________________________

1. **Research the procedure and specifications for inspecting and measuring ring gear runout in the appropriate service information.**
    a. **Maximum allowable ring gear runout: ____________ in/mm**
    b. **Type of drive axle: Integral/Unitized or Removable Carrier (Circle one)**
    c. **Does this vehicle have a removable rear differential cover? Yes/No (Circle one)**

2. **Following the specified procedure, remove the appropriate components to gain access to the ring gear assembly.**

3. **Visually inspect the ring gear for wear and damage. List your observation(s):**

4. **Using a dial indicator, measure the ring gear runout: ____________ in/mm**

5. **Determine any necessary action(s):**

6. **Have your supervisor/instructor verify satisfactory completion of this procedure, any observations found, and any necessary action(s) recommended.**

Performance Rating

CDX Tasksheet Number: C780

☐	☐	☐	☐	☐
0	1	2	3	4

Supervisor/instructor signature ______________________________________ Date ____________

▶ TASK Remove, inspect, reinstall, and/or replace drive pinion and ring gear, spacers, sleeves, and bearings.

MAST 3E1:7

Time off__________

Time on__________

Total time__________

CDX Tasksheet Number: C890

1. **Research the procedure and specifications for removing, inspecting, and replacing the drive pinion and ring gear in the appropriate service information.**
    a. **Ring gear bolt torque: __________ ft-lb/N·m**
    b. **List any special tools required for this task:**
    c. **List, or print off and attach to this sheet, the steps to perform this task:**
2. **Following the specified procedure, remove the drive pinion and ring gear.**
3. **Inspect the following components for wear or damage. List your observations for each.**
    a. **Drive pinion:**
    b. **Ring gear:**
    c. **Spacers and sleeves:**
    d. **Bearings:**

4. **Determine any necessary action(s):**

5. **Have your supervisor/instructor verify satisfactory completion of this procedure, any observations found, and any necessary action(s) recommended.**

Performance Rating

CDX Tasksheet Number: C890

0	1	2	3	4

Supervisor/instructor signature ______________________ Date ________

Time off________

Time on________

Total time________

▶ TASK Disassemble, inspect, measure, adjust, and/or replace differential pinion gears (spiders), shaft, side gears, side bearings, thrust washers, and case.

MAST 3E1:12

CDX Tasksheet Number: C147

1. **Research the procedure and specifications for disassembling, inspecting, measuring, and replacing the differential gears and associated parts.**
   a. **List any measurements or specifications for this task:**

   b. **List any special tools required for this task:**

   c. **List, or print off and attach to this sheet, the steps for performing this task:**

2. **Following the specified procedure, disassemble the differential pinion gears and associated parts.**

3. **Inspect and measure the following parts. List your observations for each.**
   a. **Differential pinion gears:**

   b. **Shaft:**

   c. **Side gears:**

d. Side bearings:

e. Thrust washers:

f. Case:

4. Determine any necessary action(s):

5. Have your supervisor/instructor verify satisfactory completion of this procedure, any observations found, and any necessary action(s) recommended.

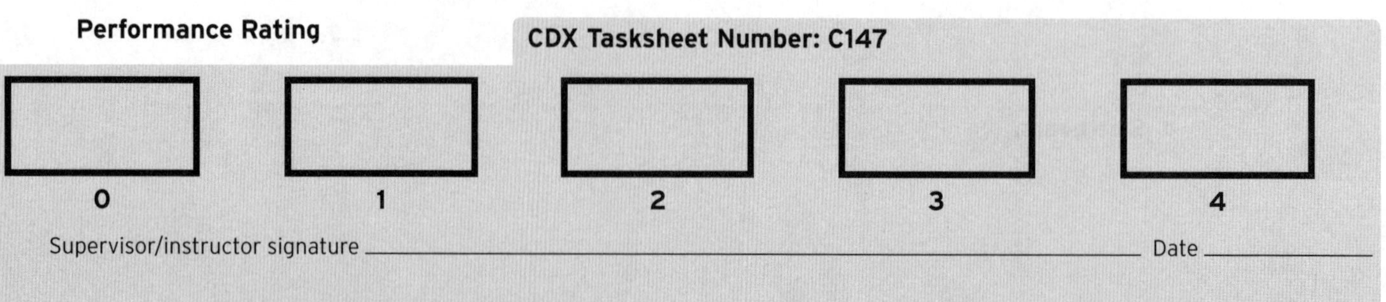

▶ TASK Measure and adjust drive pinion depth.

MAST 3E1:8

Time off________

Time on________

Total time________

CDX Tasksheet Number: C781

1. **Research the procedure and specifications for measuring and adjusting drive pinion depth in the appropriate service information.**
   a. **Specified drive pinion depth: ____________ in/N·m**
   b. **How is the drive pinion depth adjusted on this drive axle?**
   c. **List any special tools required for this task:**
   d. **List, or print off and attach to this sheet, the steps to perform this task:**
2. **Following the specified procedure, measure the drive pinion depth: ____________ in/N·m**
   a. **Is this within specifications? Yes: _____ No: _____**
3. **If outside of specifications, adjust the drive pinion depth.**
   a. **Final measurement: ____________ in/N·m**
4. **Have your supervisor/instructor verify satisfactory completion of this procedure, any observations found, and any necessary action(s) recommended.**

Performance Rating

CDX Tasksheet Number: C781

☐	☐	☐	☐	☐
0	1	2	3	4

Supervisor/instructor signature ____________________ Date ________

▶ TASK Measure and adjust drive pinion bearing preload.

MAST
3E1:9

Time off________

Time on________

Total time________

CDX Tasksheet Number: C782

1. **Research the procedure and specifications for measuring and adjusting drive pinion preload in the appropriate service information.**
   a. **Specified drive pinion preload: ________________ in-lb/N·m**
   b. **How is the drive pinion preload adjusted on this drive axle?**

   c. **List any special tools required for this task:**

2. **Following the specified procedure, measure the drive pinion preload: ________________ in-lb/N·m**
   a. **Is this within specifications? Yes: ______ No: ______**
3. **If outside of specifications, adjust the drive pinion preload.**
   a. **Final measurement: ________________ in-lb/N·m**
4. **Have your supervisor/instructor verify satisfactory completion of this procedure, any observations found, and any necessary action(s) recommended.**

Performance Rating

CDX Tasksheet Number: C782

☐	☐	☐	☐	☐
0	1	2	3	4

Supervisor/instructor signature ______________________________ Date __________

▶ TASK Reassemble and reinstall differential case assembly; measure runout; determine needed action.

MAST 3E1:13

Time off________

Time on________

Total time________

CDX Tasksheet Number: C148

1. **Research the procedure and specifications for reassembling the differential case assembly in the appropriate service information.**
   a. **Specified maximum differential case runout: ____________ in/mm**
   b. **List, or print off and attach to this sheet, any other specifications for this task:**

2. **Following the specified procedure, reassemble and reinstall the differential case assembly.**

3. **Measure the differential case runout: ____________ in/mm**

4. **Determine any necessary action(s):**

5. **Have your supervisor/instructor verify satisfactory completion of this procedure, any observations found, and any necessary action(s) recommended.**

Performance Rating

CDX Tasksheet Number: C148

☐	☐	☐	☐	☐
0	1	2	3	4

Supervisor/instructor signature ____________________ Date ________

▶ TASK Measure and adjust side bearing preload and ring and pinion gear total backlash and backlash variation on a differential carrier assembly (threaded cup or shim types).

MAST 3E1:10

Time off________

Time on________

Total time________

CDX Tasksheet Number: C145

1. **Research the procedure and specifications to measure and adjust backlash on a differential carrier assembly in the appropriate service information.**
   a. **Side bearing preload: ____________ in-lb/N·m**
   b. **Ring and pinion gear total backlash: ____________ in/mm**
   c. **Backlash variation: ____________ in/mm**
   d. **List, or print off and attach to this sheet, the steps to perform this task:**

2. **Following the specified procedure, perform the following measurements.**
   a. **Side bearing preload: ____________ in-lb/N·m**
   b. **Ring and pinion gear total backlash: ____________ in/mm**
   c. **Backlash variation: ____________ in/mm**

3. **Determine any necessary action(s):**

4. **If outside of specifications, adjust the preload and backlash. List your final measurements.**
   a. **Side bearing preload: ____________ in-lb/N·m**
   b. **Ring and pinion gear total backlash: ____________ in/mm**
   c. **Backlash variation: ____________ in/mm**

5. **Have your supervisor/instructor verify satisfactory completion of this procedure, any observations found, and any necessary action(s) recommended.**

Performance Rating

CDX Tasksheet Number: C145

0	1	2	3	4
☐	☐	☐	☐	☐

Supervisor/instructor signature ____________________ Date ________

▶ TASK Check ring and pinion tooth contact patterns; perform needed action.

MAST 3E1:11

Time off________

Time on________

Total time________

CDX Tasksheet Number: C783

1. **Research the procedure and specifications to check and correct ring and pinion gear tooth patterns in the appropriate service information.**
   a. **Draw, or print off and attach to this sheet, the correct ring and pinion gear tooth pattern for both the drive and coast sides:**

2. **Following the specified procedure, check the ring and pinion gear tooth patterns. List your observations:**

3. **Determine any necessary action(s):**

4. **Have your supervisor/instructor verify your observations. Supervisor's/instructor's initials: ________**

5. **Perform any necessary action(s). List your observation(s):**

6. **Do the patterns meet specifications? Yes: ____ No: ____**

7. **Have your supervisor/instructor verify satisfactory completion of this procedure, any observations found, and any necessary action(s) recommended.**

Performance Rating

CDX Tasksheet Number: C783

☐	☐	☐	☐	☐
0	1	2	3	4

Supervisor/instructor signature ________ Date ________

▶ TASK Clean and inspect differential case; check for leaks; inspect housing vent.

MAST 3E1:1

Time off________

Time on________

Total time________

CDX Tasksheet Number: C785

Vehicle used for this activity:

Year ________ Make ______________ Model ______________

Odometer ____________ VIN ________________________

1. **Research the procedure and specifications for cleaning and inspecting the differential housing and vent in the appropriate service information.**
    a. **Specified lubricant and/or additive:** ______________
    b. **Differential lubricant capacity:** ________ **qt/lt**
    c. **Differential fluid service interval:** ________ **mi/km**
    d. **How is the lubricant level checked in this vehicle?**

2. **Safely raise and secure the vehicle on a hoist.**

3. **Inspect the differential housing for leaks or damage. List your observation(s):**

4. **Inspect the vent and make sure it is clear of any obstructions, and connected to its vent hose if equipped. List your observations:**

5. **Determine any necessary action(s):**

6. **Have your supervisor/instructor verify satisfactory completion of this procedure, any observations found, and any necessary action(s) recommended.**

Performance Rating

CDX Tasksheet Number: C785

☐	☐	☐	☐	☐
0	1	2	3	4

Supervisor/instructor signature _______________ Date _______________

▸ TASK Measure rotating torque; determine needed action.

MAST 3E2:2

Time off________

Time on________

Total time________

CDX Tasksheet Number: C786

1. **Research the procedure and specifications for measuring the rotating torque on the limited slip differential in the appropriate service information.**
   a. **Specified breakaway torque: ________________ ft-lb/N·m**
   b. **List, or print off and attach to this sheet, the steps for measuring the rotating torque:**

2. **Following the specified procedure, measure the rotating torque: ________ ft-lb/N·m**
   a. **Is this within specifications? Yes/No (Circle one)**

3. **Determine any necessary action(s):**

4. **Have your supervisor/instructor verify satisfactory completion of this procedure, any observations found, and any necessary action(s) recommended.**

Performance Rating

CDX Tasksheet Number: C786

0	1	2	3	4
☐	☐	☐	☐	☐

Supervisor/instructor signature ________________________________ Date ____________

▶ TASK Diagnose noise, vibration, and unusual steering concerns; determine needed action.

MAST 3F5

Time off________

Time on________

Total time________

CDX Tasksheet Number: C787

1. **List the four-wheel drive/all-wheel drive steering-related customer concern:**

2. **Research the concern in the appropriate service information and list the possible causes:**

3. **Following the specified procedure, diagnose the fault. List your tests and observations:**

4. **List the cause of the noise, vibration, or steering concern:**

5. **Determine any necessary action(s) to correct the fault:**

6. **Have your supervisor/instructor verify satisfactory completion of this procedure, any observations found, and any necessary action(s) recommended.**

Performance Rating

CDX Tasksheet Number: C787

0	1	2	3	4

Supervisor/instructor signature ______________________ Date ________

▶ TASK Identify concerns related to variations in tire circumference and/or final drive ratios.

MAST 3F4

Time off________

Time on________

Total time________

CDX Tasksheet Number: C613

1. **Research the effects of variations in tire circumference and final drive ratios on the operation of a four-wheel drive/all-wheel drive vehicle in the appropriate service information.**

2. **What would the customer concern be for a four-wheel drive/all-wheel drive vehicle equipped with different size tires?**

3. **What would the customer concern be for a vehicle equipped with different final drive ratios?**

4. **Set the tire pressure to the specified pressure. Measure the tire circumference for each tire and list below:**
   a. **Left front tire circumference: ________ in/mm**
   b. **Right front tire circumference: ________ in/mm**
   c. **Right rear tire circumference: ________ in/mm**
   d. **Left rear tire circumference: ________ in/mm**

5. **How much difference in circumference is generally allowable? ________ in/mm**

6. **Determine the final drive ratios for each axle assembly:**
   a. **Rear axle ratio: ________**
   b. **Front axle ratio: ________**

7. **Determine any necessary action(s):**

8. **Have your supervisor/instructor verify satisfactory completion of this procedure, any observations found, and any necessary action(s) recommended.**

Performance Rating

CDX Tasksheet Number: C613

0	1	2	3	4
☐	☐	☐	☐	☐

Supervisor/instructor signature ________ Date ________

▶ TASK Diagnose, test, adjust, and/or replace electrical/electronic components of four-wheel drive/all-wheel drive systems.

MAST 3F6

Time off__________

Time on__________

Total time__________

CDX Tasksheet Number: C878

Vehicle used for this activity:

Year __________ Make ____________________ Model____________________

Odometer________________ VIN____________________________________

1. **List the related customer concern:**

2. **Research the possible cause(s) of the concern in the appropriate service information. List the possible cause(s):**

3. **Following the specified procedure, diagnose the cause of the concern. List your tests and observation(s):**

4. **List the cause of the concern:**

5. **Determine any necessary action(s) to correct the fault:**

6. **Have your supervisor/instructor verify satisfactory completion of this procedure, any observations found, and any necessary action(s) recommended.**

Performance Rating

CDX Tasksheet Number: C878

☐	☐	☐	☐	☐
0	1	2	3	4

Supervisor/instructor signature ______________________________ Date __________

▶ TASK Inspect, adjust, and repair shifting controls (mechanical, electrical, and vacuum), bushings, mounts, levers, and brackets.

MAST 3F1

Time off________

Time on________

Total time________

CDX Tasksheet Number: C788

1. **Research the procedure and specifications for inspecting, adjusting, and repairing the shifting controls in the appropriate service information.**
   a. **What type of controls does this vehicle use?** ________________
   b. **List or print off and attach to this sheet the steps to inspect and adjust the four-wheel drive shift controls:**

2. **Safely raise and support the vehicle on a hoist and inspect the following. List your observations for each.**
   a. **Linkage:**

   b. **Bushings:**

   c. **Mounts:**

   d. **Levers:**

   e. **Brackets:**

f. **Electric controls (if equipped):**

g. **Vacuum controls (if equipped):**

3. **Determine any necessary action(s):**

4. **Have your supervisor/instructor verify satisfactory completion of this procedure, any observations found, and any necessary action(s) recommended.**

Performance Rating

CDX Tasksheet Number: C788

0	1	2	3	4
☐	☐	☐	☐	☐

Supervisor/instructor signature ______________________ Date ________

▶ TASK Check for leaks at drive assembly and transfer case seals; check vents; check fluid level; use proper fluid type per manufacturer specification.

MAST 3F3

Time off________

Time on________

Total time________

CDX Tasksheet Number: C914

1. **Research the procedure and specifications for this task in the appropriate service information.**
    a. **List the specified lube for the drive axle:** ________________
    b. **List the specified fluid for the transfer case:** ________________
2. **Following the specified procedure, perform a visual inspection of the drive assembly seals and vents. List your observation(s) for each.**
    a. **Drive assembly seals:**
    b. **Vents:**
3. **Following the specified procedure, check the level of the drive axle lubricant. List your observations:**
4. **Following the specified procedure, perform a visual inspection of the transfer case assembly seals and vents. List your observation(s) for each.**
    a. **Transfer case seals:**
    b. **Vents:**

5. **Following the specified procedure, check the level of the transfer case fluid. List your observations:**

6. **Have your supervisor/instructor verify satisfactory completion of this procedure, any observations found, and any necessary action(s) recommended.**

Performance Rating

CDX Tasksheet Number: C914

0	1	2	3	4
☐	☐	☐	☐	☐

Supervisor/instructor signature ______________________ Date ________

▶ TASK Disassemble, service, and reassemble transfer case and components.

MAST 3F7

Time off________

Time on________

Total time________

CDX Tasksheet Number: C875

1. **Research the procedure and specifications for disassembling, servicing, and reassembling the transfer case in the appropriate service information.**
   a. **List any special tools required for this task:**

   b. **List the flat rate time for this task: ________________ hr**
   c. **List or print off and attach to this sheet the steps to disassemble and reassemble the transfer case:**

2. **Following the specified procedure, disassemble the transfer case.**

> NOTE It is good practice to lay out the components on a workbench or parts tray in a logical manner to facilitate reassembly.

3. **Following the specified procedure, inspect the components for wear or damage. List your observations:**

4. **Determine any necessary action(s):**

5. **Have your supervisor/instructor verify disassembly and observations. Supervisor's/instructor's initials: ____________________**

6. **Following the specified procedure, service the transfer case components and list your actions:**

7. **Have your supervisor/instructor verify that the transfer case is ready to be reassembled and initial below.**

    a. **Supervisor's/instructor's initials: ____________________**

8. **Following the specified procedure, reassemble the transfer case. Be sure to tighten all fasteners to the proper torque. List your observations:**

9. **Have your supervisor/instructor verify satisfactory completion of this procedure, any observations found, and any necessary action(s) recommended.**

Performance Rating

CDX Tasksheet Number: C875

☐	☐	☐	☐	☐
0	1	2	3	4

Supervisor/instructor signature ______________________________ Date __________

▶ TASK Inspect locking hubs; determine needed action(s).

MAST 3F2

Time off________

Time on________

Total time________

CDX Tasksheet Number: C876

1. **Research the procedure and specifications for servicing the wheel bearings and locking hubs in the appropriate service information.**
   a. **List the specified wheel-bearing lubricant:** ____________________
   b. **List or print off and attach to this sheet the procedure for adjusting the wheel bearings:**

2. **Safely raise and support the vehicle on a hoist or jack stands.**

3. **Following the specified procedure, remove the locking hub(s) and wheel bearings (inner and outer). List your observation(s):**

4. **Following the specified procedure, disassemble the locking hub(s). Clean all parts in an environmentally safe way and re-inspect each component. List your observation(s):**

> NOTE There are various views on whether a wheel bearing should be cleaned with solvents, as it could leave solvent-laden grease in the bearing. See your instructor or the service information for the recommended procedure for cleaning and packing wheel bearings.

5. **Determine any necessary action(s):**

6. **Have your supervisor/instructor verify disassembly and observations. Supervisor's/instructor's initials:** ____________________

7. **Following the specified procedure, repack the wheel bearings and lubricate the locking hub components.**

8. **Following the specified procedure, reassemble the wheel bearings. Make sure you properly adjust the wheel bearings.**

> **NOTE** Most wheel bearings require a three-step adjustment procedure. First, apply a large initial torque to the wheel-bearing adjustment nut to seat the wheel bearings. Second, back off the adjustment nut. Third, readjust with a much smaller torque to provide the proper bearing preload. Do not leave the bearings torqued to the higher torque or damage to the bearings will result. Also, remember to use a new cotter pin if that is the method used to retain the adjustment nut.

9. **Have your supervisor/instructor verify correct bearing adjustment. Supervisor's/instructor's initials:** ____________________

10. **Following the specified procedure, reassemble the locking hubs. List your observation(s):**

11. **Have your supervisor/instructor verify satisfactory completion of this procedure, any observations found, and any necessary action(s) recommended.**

Performance Rating

CDX Tasksheet Number: C876

☐	☐	☐	☐	☐
0	1	2	3	4

Supervisor/instructor signature ____________________ Date __________

▶ TASK Research vehicle service information, fluid type, vehicle service history, service precautions, and technical service bulletins.

MAST 2A2

Time off________

Time on________

Total time________

CDX Tasksheet Number: C681

1. **Using the vehicle VIN for identification, use the appropriate source to access the vehicle's service history in relation to prior related transmission/transaxle work or customer concerns.**
   a. **List any transmission-related repairs/concerns, and their dates:**

2. **List the specified type of fluid for this vehicle:**

   ____

3. **Using the vehicle VIN for identification, access any relevant technical service bulletins for the particular vehicle you are working on in relation to any transmission/transaxle updates, precautions, or other service issues. List any related service bulletins and their titles:**

4. **Have your supervisor/instructor verify satisfactory completion of this procedure, any observations found, and any necessary action(s) recommended.**

Performance Rating

CDX Tasksheet Number: C681

☐	☐	☐	☐	☐
0	1	2	3	4

Supervisor/instructor signature ____________________ Date ________

▶ TASK Demonstrate the use of the three Cs (concern, cause, and correction).

Additional Task

Time off________

Time on________

Total time________

CDX Tasksheet Number: N/A

1. **Using the following scenario, write up the three Cs as listed on most repair orders. Assume that the customer authorized the recommended repairs.**

   A compact vehicle is brought to your shop with an automatic transaxle concern. The customer tells you that the transmission started slipping a couple of days ago, and it is getting worse. You road test the vehicle and notice that it is slipping in all gears when under moderate load. You pull the vehicle onto a rack and find the following:

   a. **The vehicle has 122,000 miles on it, but is in good condition otherwise.**
   b. **The transmission fluid is dark and smells burnt. The fluid is about two pints too low, but topping it off does not stop the vehicle from slipping when it is stall-tested.**
   c. **The transmission-pan gasket and both axle seals are seeping heavily.**
   d. **With the pan removed, there is a lot of band and clutch material in the bottom, but very few metal filings.**
   e. **The transmission mount is torn.**
   f. **Both outer CV joint boots are badly cracked and just starting to leak grease, but the joints are still good.**

> NOTE Ask your instructor whether you should use a copy of the shop repair order or the three Cs here to record this information.

2. **Concern:**

3. **Cause:**

4. **Correction:**

5. **Other recommended service:**

6. **Have your supervisor/instructor verify satisfactory completion of this task, any observations found, and any necessary action(s) recommended.**

Performance Rating

CDX Tasksheet Number: N/A

0	1	2	3	4

Supervisor/instructor signature ______________________________ Date __________

Time off________

Time on________

Total time________

▶ TASK Diagnose pressure concerns in a transmission using hydraulic principles (Pascal's Law).

MAST 2A12

CDX Tasksheet Number: C747

Vehicle used for this activity:

Year ____________ Make ________________________ Model ________________________

Odometer ____________________ VIN ____

1. **List the transmission/transaxle pressure-related concern:**

2. **Research the concern in the appropriate service information.**
   a. **List the possible cause(s) of the concern:**

   b. **List (or print off and attach) any specified transmission pressures:**

3. **Write out Pascal's Law in your own words:**

4. **Describe how you will use Pascal's Law to help you diagnose this concern:**

5. **Perform the appropriate pressure tests and list your observation(s):**

6. **Determine any necessary action(s) to correct the fault:**

7. **Have your supervisor/instructor verify satisfactory completion of this procedure, any observations found, and any necessary action(s) recommended.**

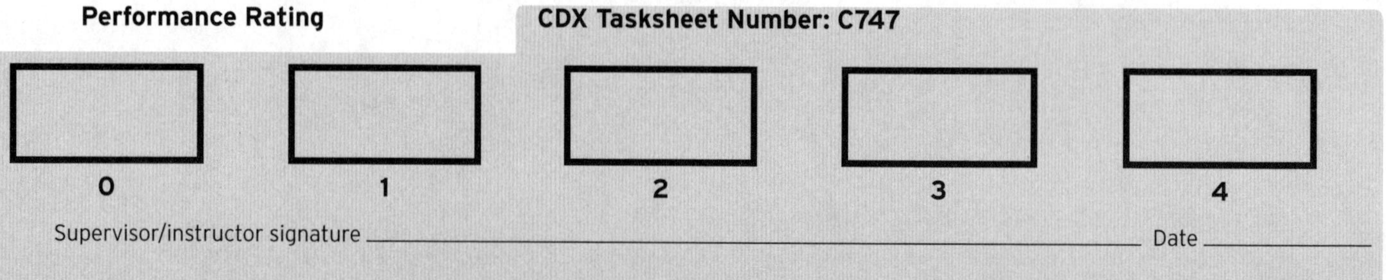
Performance Rating

CDX Tasksheet Number: C747

0	1	2	3	4

Supervisor/instructor signature ______________________ Date __________

▶ TASK Diagnose transmission/transaxle gear reduction/multiplication concerns using driving, driven, and held-member (power flow) principles.

MAST 2A10

Time off__________

Time on__________

Total time__________

CDX Tasksheet Number: C066

Vehicle used for this activity:

Year ________ Make ______________ Model______________

Odometer____________ VIN______________________

1. **List the customer concern:**

2. **Research the particular transmission/transaxle concern in the appropriate service information, including power flow charts and driving, driven, and held-member charts.**
   a. **List the possible cause(s) of the concern:**

   b. **List or print off and attach to this sheet the procedure for diagnosing the concern:**

3. **Perform the diagnostic tests following the specified procedure.**
   a. **List your tests and test results:**

b. Describe how you used the diagnostic charts to diagnose the concern:

4. Determine any necessary action(s) to correct the fault:

5. Have your supervisor/instructor verify satisfactory completion of this procedure, any observations found, and any necessary action(s) recommended.

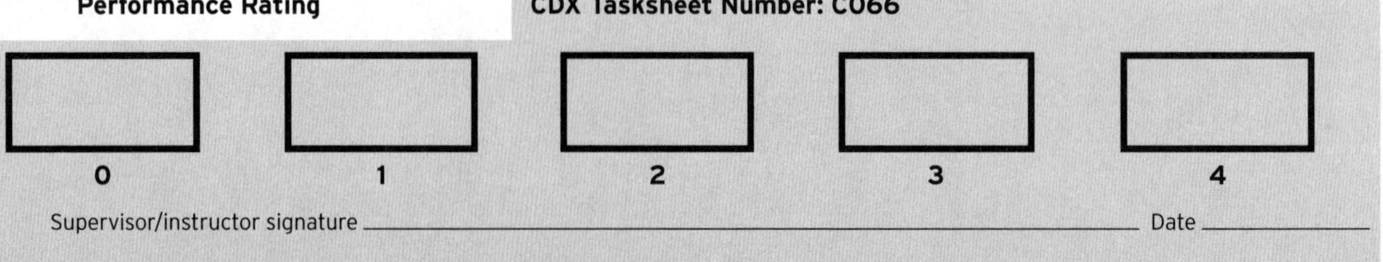

Performance Rating
CDX Tasksheet Number: C066
0
1
2
3
4
Supervisor/instructor signature
Date

▶ TASK Remove and reinstall transmission/transaxle and torque converter; inspect engine core plugs, rear crankshaft seal, dowel pins, dowel pinholes, and mating surfaces.

MAST 2C1

Time off________

Time on________

Total time________

CDX Tasksheet Number: C604

1. **Research the following torque specifications and transmission/transaxle removal and installation procedure in the appropriate service information.**
   a. **Flexplate-to-crankshaft bolt torque: ________ ft-lb/N·m**
   b. **Torque converter-to-flexplate bolt torque: ________ ft-lb/N·m**
   c. **Transmission-to-block bolt torque: ________ ft-lb/N·m**
   d. **Transmission fluid type: ________**
   e. **Transmission fluid capacity: ________ qt/lt**
   f. **List or print off and attach to this sheet the procedure for removing and installing the transmission/transaxle:**

2. **Following the specified procedure, remove the transmission/transaxle from the vehicle.**

3. **Inspect the following components and list your observations.**
   a. **Engine core plugs:**

   b. **Rear crankshaft seal:**

   c. **Dowel pins and holes:**

   d. **Engine and bell-housing mating surfaces:**

4. Have your supervisor/instructor verify your observations. Supervisor's/instructor's initials:______________________

> **NOTE** At this time, you may want to overhaul the transmission/transaxle or perform other tasks such as inspecting/replacing the torque converter or flushing the transmission/transaxle cooler lines. Once any related tasks are completed and it is time to reinstall the transmission/transaxle, return to this page to complete the task and have it signed off.

5. **Prepare the transmission to be reinstalled. Ensure that the torque converter is fully engaged in the transmission. Failure to do so may cause severe damage to the transmission/transaxle and the converter.**

6. **Have your instructor check that the converter is installed properly. Supervisor's/instructor's initials: ______________________**

7. **Position all wires, hoses, and tubes out of the way and in their specified positions. Secure them temporarily if necessary.**

> **NOTE** It is easy for wires and hoses to fall down and get pinched between the engine and bell housing. This will cause electrical issues in the vehicle as well as alignment issues with the transmission.

8. **Following the specified procedure, reinstall the transmission/transaxle. Be sure to tighten all fasteners to the proper torque.**

9. **Refill the transmission/transaxle to the proper level.**

10. **Check that all cooler lines, electrical wires, linkages, and other removed components are properly installed and adjusted.**

11. **Have your instructor verify that the vehicle is ready to be started. Supervisor's/instructor's initials: ______________________**

12. **Place exhaust hose(s) over the exhaust pipe(s) and set the parking brake.**

13. **Start the vehicle and move the transmission selector through each gear. Check the transmission fluid level and top off as necessary.**

14. **Check for leaks, loose parts, or anything that isn't right with the transmission and the related parts. List your observation(s):**

15. **With your supervisor's/instructor's permission, test drive the vehicle to ensure the transmission operates correctly. List your observations:**

16. Double check your work and verify that there are no leaks and that everything is back in its proper place. List your observations:

17. Have your supervisor/instructor verify satisfactory completion of this procedure, any observations found, and any necessary action(s) recommended.

Performance Rating

CDX Tasksheet Number: C604

0	1	2	3	4

Supervisor/instructor signature ______________________ Date ________

▶ TASK Inspect converter flex (drive) plate, converter-attaching bolts, converter pilot, converter pump-drive surfaces, converter end play, and crankshaft pilot bore.

MAST 2C3

Time off________

Time on________

Total time________

CDX Tasksheet Number: C605

1. **Research the procedure and specifications for inspecting the torque converter, flexplate, and crankshaft pilot bore.**
   a. **Torque converter-to-flexplate bolt torque: ________ ft-lb/N·m**
   b. **Flexplate-to-crankshaft bolt torque: ________ ft-lb/N·m**
   c. **Converter end play: ________ in/mm**
   d. **Converter pilot diameter, if specified: ________ in/mm**
   e. **Crankshaft pilot bore, if specified: ________ in/mm**

2. **Following the specified procedure, inspect each of the listed items below. List your observations.**
   a. **Flexplate (cracks, warpage, elongated holes, starter ring-gear wear, etc.):**

   b. **Converter-attaching bolts (worn, stretched, rounded heads, etc.):**

   c. **Converter pilot (gouges, excessive rust, etc.):**

   d. **Crankshaft pilot bore (gouges, excessive rust, etc.):**

   e. **Converter pump-drive surface (wear, nicks, burrs, etc.):**

   f. **Converter end play: ________ in/mm**

3. **Determine any necessary action(s):**

4. **Have your supervisor/instructor verify satisfactory completion of this procedure, any observations found, and any necessary action(s) recommended.**

Performance Rating

CDX Tasksheet Number: C605

0	1	2	3	4
☐	☐	☐	☐	☐

Supervisor/instructor signature _______________ Date _______

▶ TASK Inspect, leak test, flush and/or replace transmission/transaxle oil cooler, lines, and fittings.

MAST 2C2

Time off__________

Time on__________

Total time__________

CDX Tasksheet Number: C749

1. **Research the procedure to inspect, test, flush, and replace the cooler lines and fittings.**
   a. **List or print off and attach to this sheet the steps to test, flush, and replace the cooler lines:**

2. **Following the specified procedure, perform the following tasks. List your observations.**
   a. **Inspect the cooler, lines, and fittings for damage or wear:**

   b. **Test the cooler, lines, and fittings for leaks:**

   c. **Flush or replace the cooler and lines:**

3. **Have your supervisor/instructor verify satisfactory completion of this procedure, any observations found, and any necessary action(s) recommended.**

Performance Rating

CDX Tasksheet Number: C749

☐	☐	☐	☐	☐
0	1	2	3	4

Supervisor/instructor signature ____________________ Date __________

▶ TASK Measure transmission/transaxle end play and/or preload; determine needed action.

MAST
2C11

Time off________

Time on________

Total time________

CDX Tasksheet Number: C689

1. **Research the procedure and specifications to measure the end play or preload.**
   a. **Specified end play or preload:** ________________
   b. **List, or print off and attach to this sheet, the steps to perform the end play or preload measurement:**

   c. **How is the end play or preload adjusted on this transmission/transaxle?**

2. **Following the specified procedure, measure the end play or preload:**

   ____

3. **Determine any necessary action(s):**

4. **Have your supervisor/instructor verify satisfactory completion of this procedure, any observations found, and any necessary action(s) recommended.**

Performance Rating

CDX Tasksheet Number: C689

0	1	2	3	4

Supervisor/instructor signature ________________ Date ________

▶ TASK Disassemble, clean, and inspect transmission/transaxle.

MAST 2C6

Time off________

Time on________

Total time________

CDX Tasksheet Number: C684

1. **Research the disassembly and inspection procedures in the appropriate service information.**
   a. **List any precautions for performing this task:**

   b. **List any special tools required to perform this task:**

2. **Following the specified procedure, disassemble the transmission/transaxle into its unit components, ensuring that you note their location and orientation. Make notes or take pictures as appropriate. Also, lay them out in a logical manner to facilitate reassembly.**

> NOTE Round objects such as clutch drums, ball bearings, roller bearings, and bushings can roll off of the work table if not secured, causing personal injury. This could also lead to damage or loss of the components. Always lay round objects on their side when possible, or store them in a work tray to prevent rolling.

3. **Clean the components according to the specified procedure. Make sure you relocate them in the same logical sequence as before**

4. **Perform a preliminary visual inspection of the components. This is an initial inspection designed to identify major issues with the transmission/transaxle. Further inspection of the subunits will occur later. List your observations for each main assembly:**

5. **Have your supervisor/instructor verify satisfactory completion of this procedure, any observations found, and any necessary action(s) recommended.**

Performance Rating

CDX Tasksheet Number: C684

0	1	2	3	4

Supervisor/instructor signature _______________ Date _______

▶ TASK Inspect, measure, and reseal oil pump assembly and components. MAST 2C10

Time off________

Time on________

Total time________

CDX Tasksheet Number: C688

1. **Research the procedure for disassembling and inspecting the oil pump in the appropriate service information.**
   a. **Type of pump (gerotor, crescent, vane, etc.):** ____________________
   b. **List, or print off and attach to this sheet, the clearance specifications for this pump:**

   c. **Pump housing bolt torque:** ____________________ **ft-lb/N·m**
   d. **Pump-to-case bolt torque:** ____________________ **ft-lb/N·m**

2. **Following the specified procedure, disassemble the oil pump. Be sure not to damage any of the surfaces or parts.**

> NOTE You may need to scribe a mark on the pump halves so that you can reassemble the pump in the proper orientation. Refer to the service information to see if this is the case. Also be careful not to damage any of the wear surfaces with a scribe. Use a nondamaging method of marking the components.

3. **Measure the specified clearances. List your readings:**

4. **Determine any necessary action(s):**

5. **Have your supervisor/instructor verify disassembly.**
   Supervisor's/instructor's initials: ____________________

6. **Following the specified procedure, reassemble the oil pump. Be sure to prelubricate the oil pump and replace any seals and bushings as necessary. List your observations:**

7. **Have your supervisor/instructor verify satisfactory completion of this procedure, any observations found, and any necessary action(s) recommended.**

Performance Rating

CDX Tasksheet Number: C688

0	1	2	3	4
☐	☐	☐	☐	☐

Supervisor/instructor signature ____________________ Date __________

▶ TASK Inspect and measure planetary gear assembly components; determine needed action.

MAST 2C15

Time off________

Time on________

Total time________

CDX Tasksheet Number: C752

1. **Research the procedure for inspecting and measuring the planetary gear(s) in the appropriate service information.**
    a. **Type of planetary gear (Simpson, Ravigneaux, etc.):** ________________
    b. **List, or print off and attach to this sheet, the clearance and other specifications for the planetary gear(s):**

2. **Following the specified procedure, perform any planetary gear assembly measurements. List your observations:**

3. **Visually inspect the planetary gear assemblies (including the sun gear, ring gear, planetary gears, thrust washers, and carrier assembly) for wear or damage. List your observations:**

4. **Determine any necessary action(s):**

5. **Have your supervisor/instructor verify satisfactory completion of this procedure, any observations found, and any necessary action(s) recommended.**

Performance Rating

CDX Tasksheet Number: C752

0	1	2	3	4
☐	☐	☐	☐	☐

Supervisor/instructor signature ________________ Date ________

▶ TASK Inspect bushings; determine needed action.

MAST
2C14

Time off________

Time on________

Total time________

CDX Tasksheet Number: C751

1. **Research the procedure and any specifications for inspecting the bushings in the appropriate service information.**
   a. **List the name and any specifications for each bushing:**

2. **Following the specified procedure, inspect and/or measure each bushing. List your observations:**

3. **Determine any necessary action(s):**

4. **Have your supervisor/instructor verify satisfactory completion of this procedure, any observations found, and any necessary action(s) recommended.**

Performance Rating

CDX Tasksheet Number: C751

☐	☐	☐	☐	☐
0	1	2	3	4

Supervisor/instructor signature ________________________________ Date ____________

▶ TASK Inspect, measure, and/or replace thrust washers and bearings.

MAST 2C12

Time off__________

Time on__________

Total time__________

CDX Tasksheet Number: C750

1. **Research the procedure and specifications for inspecting, measuring, and replacing thrust washers and bearings in the appropriate service information.**
   a. **List the name and specified thickness for each thrust washer and thrust bearing:**

   b. **Which thrust washer(s) or thrust bearing(s) is the selective fit for obtaining the proper gear train end play?**

2. **Following the specified procedure, inspect and/or measure each thrust washer and thrust bearing. List your observations:**

3. **Determine any necessary action(s):**

4. **Have your supervisor/instructor verify satisfactory completion of this procedure, any observations found, and any necessary action(s) recommended.**

Performance Rating

CDX Tasksheet Number: C750

0	1	2	3	4

Supervisor/instructor signature ____________________ Date __________

▶ **TASK** Inspect one-way clutches, races, rollers, sprags, springs, cages, and retainers; determine needed action.

MAST 2C22

Time off_______

Time on_______

Total time_______

CDX Tasksheet Number: C759

1. **Research the procedure and any specifications for inspecting the one-way clutch assemblies in the appropriate service information.**
   a. **List the device that each roller or sprag clutch holds:**

   b. **List, or print off and attach to this sheet, any inspection procedures for these components:**

2. **Following the specified procedure, inspect each one-way clutch (including races, rollers, sprags, springs, cages, and retainers). List your observations:**

3. **Determine any necessary action(s):**

4. **Have your supervisor/instructor verify satisfactory completion of this procedure, any observations found, and any necessary action(s) recommended.**

Performance Rating

CDX Tasksheet Number: C759

☐	☐	☐	☐	☐
0	1	2	3	4

Supervisor/instructor signature _______________ Date _______

TASK Inspect oil delivery circuits, including seal rings, ring grooves, and sealing surface areas, feed pipes, orifices, and check valves/balls. **MAST 2C13**

Time off________

Time on________

Total time________

CDX Tasksheet Number: C690

1. **Research the procedure and any specifications for inspecting the oil delivery circuits, including seal rings, ring grooves, and sealing surface areas; feed pipes; orifices; and check valves/balls.**
   a. **List any specifications for the above components:**

2. **Following the specified procedure, inspect the oil delivery circuits (including the components above). List your observations:**

3. **Determine any necessary action(s):**

4. **Have your supervisor/instructor verify satisfactory completion of this procedure, any observations found, and any necessary action(s) recommended.**

Performance Rating

CDX Tasksheet Number: C690

☐	☐	☐	☐	☐
0	1	2	3	4

Supervisor/instructor signature ________________ Date ________

▶ TASK Inspect case bores, passages, bushings, vents, and mating surfaces; determine needed action.

MAST 2C16

Time off________

Time on________

Total time________

CDX Tasksheet Number: C753

1. **Research the procedure and any specifications for inspecting case bores, passages, bushings, vents, and mating surfaces.**
   a. **List any specifications for the above components:**

2. **Following the specified procedure, inspect case bores, passages, bushings, vents, and mating surfaces. List your observations:**

3. **Determine any necessary action(s):**

4. **Have your supervisor/instructor verify satisfactory completion of this procedure, any observations found, and any necessary action(s) recommended.**

Performance Rating

CDX Tasksheet Number: C753

☐	☐	☐	☐	☐
0	1	2	3	4

Supervisor/instructor signature ________________________ Date ____________

▶ TASK Inspect clutch drum, piston, check balls, springs, retainers, seals, friction plates, pressure plates, and bands; determine needed action.

MAST 2C19

Time off______

Time on______

Total time______

CDX Tasksheet Number: C756

1. **Research the procedure and specifications for inspecting the clutch drum, piston, check balls, springs, retainers, seals, and friction and pressure plates for each clutch.**

    a. **In the table below, list the name of each clutch this transmission/ transaxle is equipped with and the number of steel plates and friction plates it contains.**

Name of Clutch	Number of Steel Plates	Number of Friction Plates

    b. **List, or print off and attach to this sheet, any specifications related to the clutch drum, piston, check balls, springs, retainers, seals, and friction and pressure plates:**

    c. **Research the procedure and specifications for inspecting the bands.**

        i. **List each band and the gear(s) each band is applied in:**

ii. **List any specifications for each band:**

2. **Following the specified procedure, disassemble and inspect the components for each clutch assembly. List your observations for each clutch:**

3. **Following the specified procedure, inspect each band for wear or damage. List your observations:**

4. **Determine any necessary action(s):**

5. **Have your supervisor/instructor verify satisfactory completion of this procedure, any observations found, and any necessary action(s) recommended.**

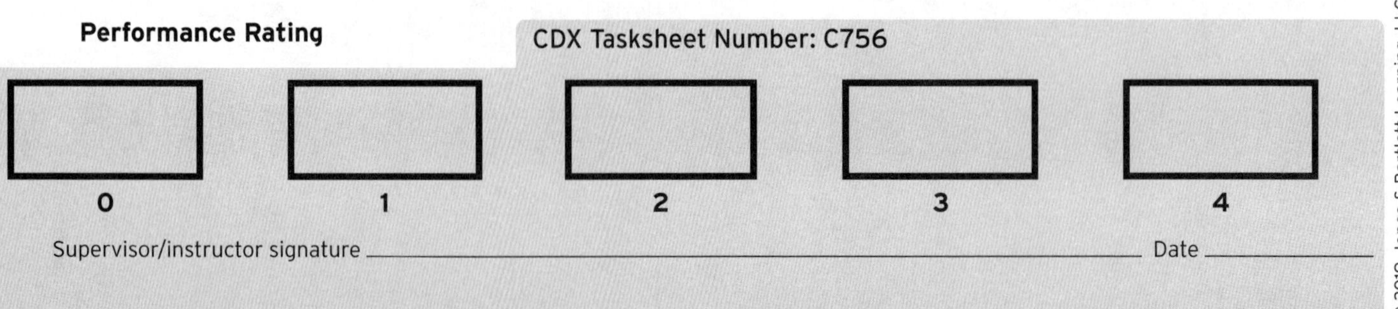

▶ TASK Measure clutch pack clearance; determine needed action.

MAST 2C20

CDX Tasksheet Number: C757

Time off________

Time on________

Total time________

1. **Research the procedure and specifications for measuring clutch pack clearance in the appropriate service information.**
   a. **List the specified clutch pack clearance for each clutch in the table below.**

Name of Clutch	Specified Clearance (in/mm)

   b. **List how each clutch pack clearance is adjusted on this transmission/ transaxle:**

2. **If not already completed, reassemble each clutch following the specified procedure.**

3. **Following the specified procedure, measure the clutch pack clearance for each clutch. List your measurements in the table below.**

Name of Clutch	Measured Clearance (in/mm)

4. **Determine any necessary action(s):**

5. **Have your supervisor/instructor verify satisfactory completion of this procedure, any observations found, and any necessary action(s) recommended.**

Performance Rating

CDX Tasksheet Number: C757

0	1	2	3	4

Supervisor/instructor signature ________ Date ________

▶ TASK Air test operation of clutch and servo assemblies.

MAST 2C21

CDX Tasksheet Number: C758

Time off___________

Time on___________

Total time___________

> **NOTE** Most clutch assemblies can usually be air tested outside of the transmission once they are completely assembled with the clutch pack. Therefore, now would be a good time to perform that task for each self-contained clutch pack. Servos, which operate bands, must usually be tested with the gear train and bands installed. You may have to come back to this task for supervisor/instructor sign-off when it is appropriate to air test any servos during the assembly of the transmission/transaxle.

1. **Research the procedure for air testing each clutch and servo assembly.**
   a. **List any special tools needed for this procedure:**

2. **Following the specified procedure, air test each clutch assembly. List your observations for each one in the table below.**

Name of Clutch	Observations

3. **Have your supervisor/instructor verify the above results. Supervisor's/instructor's initials: ___________**

4. **Once the transmission/transaxle is assembled far enough to air test the servos, test each one following the specified procedure. List your observations in the table below.**

Name of Servo	Observations

a. **Determine any necessary action(s):**

5. **Have your supervisor/instructor verify satisfactory completion of this procedure, any observations found, and any necessary action(s) recommended.**

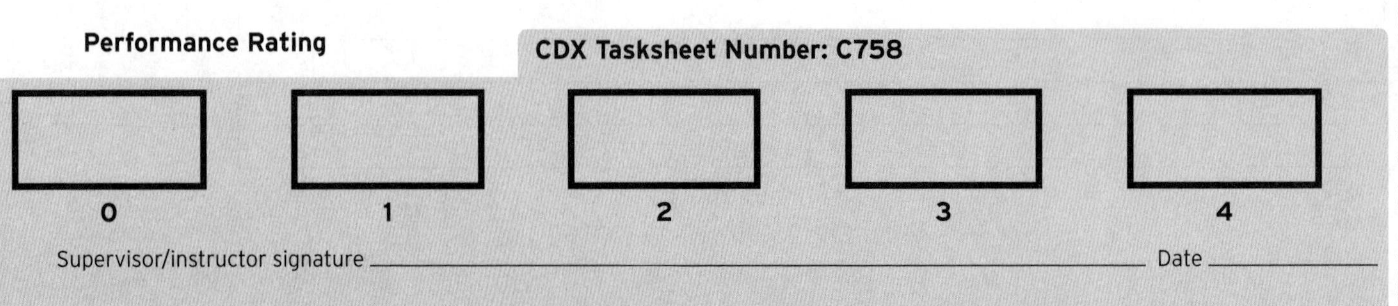

Time off________

Time on________

Total time________

▶ TASK Inspect servo and accumulator bores, pistons, seals, pins, springs, and retainers; determine needed action.

MAST 2C8

CDX Tasksheet Number: C686

1. **Research the procedure and any specifications for inspecting servo and accumulator bores, pistons, seals, pins, springs, and retainers.**
   a. **List any specifications for the above components:**

2. **If not already completed, disassemble each servo and accumulator.**

3. **Following the specified procedure, inspect servo and accumulator bores, pistons, seals, pins, springs, and retainers. List your observations:**

4. **Determine any necessary action(s):**

5. **Have your supervisor/instructor verify satisfactory completion of this procedure, any observations found, and any necessary action(s) recommended.**

Performance Rating

CDX Tasksheet Number: C686

0	1	2	3	4
☐	☐	☐	☐	☐

Supervisor/instructor signature ________________________ Date ________

▶ TASK Inspect, measure, clean, and replace valve body (includes surfaces, bores, springs, valves, switches, solenoids, sleeves, retainers, brackets, check valves/balls, screens, spacers, and gaskets). **MAST 2C7**

Time off________

Time on________

Total time________

CDX Tasksheet Number: C685

1. **Research the procedure and specifications to inspect, measure, clean, and replace the valve body.**
    a. **List, or print off and attach to this sheet, any precautions for this task:**

    b. **List, or print off and attach to this sheet, any specifications related to this task:**

    c. **List, or print off and attach to this sheet, the torque specifications for the valve body bolts, screws, and fasteners:**

2. **Following the specified procedure, disassemble, clean, measure, and inspect the valve body components. List your observations for each.**
    a. **Valve body and plate surfaces:**

    b. **Bores, valves, and sleeves:**

c. **Springs:**

d. **Retainers, spacers, and brackets:**

e. **Check valves and check balls:**

f. **Gaskets and screens:**

3. **Have your supervisor/instructor verify disassembly of the valve body. Supervisor's/instructor's initials: ____________________**

4. **Following the specified procedure, reassemble the valve body. Be careful to install all valves, springs, check balls, and gaskets in the proper orientation. Also, be sure to torque all fasteners in the correct sequence and to the proper torque.**

5. **Have your supervisor/instructor verify satisfactory completion of this procedure, any observations found, and any necessary action(s) recommended.**

Performance Rating

CDX Tasksheet Number: C685

☐	☐	☐	☐	☐
0	1	2	3	4

Supervisor/instructor signature ______________________________ Date ____________

▶ TASK Inspect, measure, repair, adjust, or replace transaxle final drive components.

MAST 2C18

Time off__________

Time on__________

Total time__________

CDX Tasksheet Number: C755

1. **Research the procedure and specifications to inspect, measure, repair, adjust, or replace transaxle final drive components.**
   a. **List, or print off and attach to this sheet, any precautions for this task:**

   b. **List any special tools required to complete this task:**

   c. **List, or print off and attach to this sheet, any specifications related to this task:**

2. **Following the specified procedure, inspect, measure, repair, adjust, or replace the following components. List your observations.**
   a. **Link chains:**

   b. **Sprockets:**

c. **Gears:**

d. **Bearings:**

e. **Bushings:**

3. **Determine any necessary action(s):**

4. **Have your supervisor/instructor verify satisfactory completion of this procedure, any observations found, and any necessary action(s) recommended.**

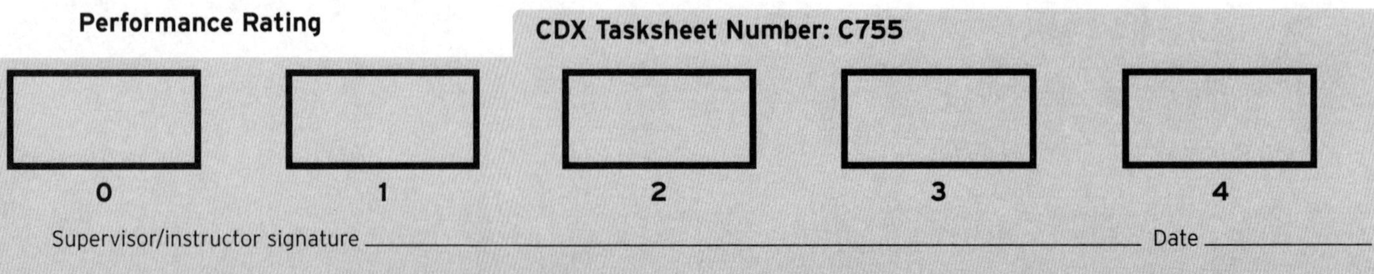

Performance Rating

CDX Tasksheet Number: C755

0 1 2 3 4

Supervisor/instructor signature ______________________ Date __________

▶ TASK Diagnose and inspect transaxle drive, link chains, sprockets, gears, bearings, and bushings; perform needed action.

Time off______

Time on______

Total time______

CDX Tasksheet Number: C754

1. **Research the procedure and specifications to inspect the transaxle drive, link chains, sprockets, gears, bearings, and bushings.**
   a. **List, or print off and attach to this sheet, any precautions for this task:**

   b. **List, or print off and attach to this sheet, any specifications related to this task:**

2. **Following the specified procedure, inspect the following components. List your observations.**
   a. **Link chains:**

   b. **Sprockets:**

   c. **Gears:**

   d. **Bearings:**

e. **Bushings:**

3. **Determine any necessary action(s):**

4. **Have your supervisor/instructor verify satisfactory completion of this procedure, any observations found, and any necessary action(s) recommended.**

Performance Rating

CDX Tasksheet Number: C754

0	1	2	3	4
☐	☐	☐	☐	☐

Supervisor/instructor signature ______________________ Date ________

▶ TASK Assemble transmission/transaxle.

MAST 2C9

Time off________

Time on________

Total time________

CDX Tasksheet Number: C083

1. **Research the reassembly procedure for this transmission/transaxle in the appropriate service information.**
   a. **List the specified assembly lubricant:**

      ____

   b. **List the special tools required to perform this task:**

   c. **Transmission/transaxle end play:** ________________________ **in/mm**

NOTE All of the component assemblies should already be properly reassembled. If they are not, reassemble them according to the specified procedures as listed in previous tasks. Ensure that they meet all specifications.

2. **Following the specified procedure, reassemble the transmission, making sure all components are seated properly. Perform all specified checks along the way. List your observations:**

3. **Once the transmission/transaxle gear train and pump are fully installed, adjust any bands if necessary.**
   a. **Air check each servo and clutch. List each clutch and servo and your observations:**

NOTE Your instructor may want to approve the servo air check from task C758, "Air test operation of clutch and servo assemblies," after you perform it here.

b. **Measure the gear train end play: ______________________ in/mm**

4. **Following the specified procedure, reinstall the valve body, linkage, filter, and pan(s).**

5. **Complete any other specified procedures related to the assembly process.**

6. **Have your supervisor/instructor verify satisfactory completion of this procedure, any observations found, and any necessary action(s) recommended.**

Performance Rating

CDX Tasksheet Number: C083

☐	☐	☐	☐	☐
0	1	2	3	4

Supervisor/instructor signature ______________________ Date ____________

▶ TASK Check fluid level in a transmission or a transaxle equipped with a dipstick.

Time off__________

Time on__________

Total time__________

CDX Tasksheet Number: C902

1. **Research the procedure to check the transmission fluid level in the appropriate service information. List the specified steps:**

2. **Following the specified steps, check the transmission fluid level. List level:**

3. **Have your supervisor/instructor verify satisfactory completion of this procedure, any observations found, and any necessary action(s) recommended.**

Performance Rating

CDX Tasksheet Number: C902

0	1	2	3	4
☐	☐	☐	☐	☐

Supervisor/instructor signature ____________________ Date __________

▶ TASK Check fluid level in a transmission or a transaxle not equipped with a dipstick.

MAST 2A5

Time off________

Time on________

Total time________

CDX Tasksheet Number: C903X

Vehicle used for this activity:

Year________ Make________________ Model________________

Odometer________________ VIN ________________

1. **Research the procedure to check the transmission fluid level in a vehicle that doesn't use a transmission dipstick in the appropriate service information. List the specified steps:**

2. **Following the specified steps, check the transmission fluid level. List level:**

3. **Have your supervisor/instructor verify satisfactory completion of this procedure, any observations found, and any necessary action(s) recommended.**

Performance Rating

CDX Tasksheet Number: C903X

☐	☐	☐	☐	☐
0	1	2	3	4

Supervisor/instructor signature ________________ Date ________

▶ TASK Diagnose fluid loss and condition concerns; determine needed action.

MAST 2A3

Time off________

Time on________

Total time________

CDX Tasksheet Number: C682

1. **List the automatic transmission fluid loss or condition concern:**

2. **Safely raise and support the vehicle on a hoist. Inspect the transmission for any fluid leaks. List the source of any leaks:**

3. **Place a few drops of transmission fluid from the transmission on a clean white paper towel. The transmission fluid should have a clean appearance on the towel. If the center portion of the fluid is dirty, then the fluid is dirty. List your observation(s):**

4. **Smell the transmission fluid. Compare it to a fresh sample of the correct transmission fluid. List your observation(s):**

5. **If the fluid is in poor condition, ask your instructor if you should change the fluid and filter. If so, inspect the bottom of the pan once it is removed. List your observation(s):**

6. **Determine any necessary actions to correct the fault(s):**

7. **Have your supervisor/instructor verify satisfactory completion of this procedure, any observations found, and any necessary action(s) recommended.**

Performance Rating | **CDX Tasksheet Number: C682**

0	1	2	3	4
☐	☐	☐	☐	☐

Supervisor/instructor signature ____________________ Date ________

▶ TASK Drain and replace fluid and filter(s); use proper fluid type per manufacturer specification.

MAST 2B4

Time off________

Time on________

Total time________

CDX Tasksheet Number: C907

Vehicle used for this activity:

Year ________ Make ________________ Model________________

Odometer____________ VIN________________________

1. **Research the specifications and procedure in the appropriate service information.**
   a. **Transmission service interval: ________________ mi/km**
   b. **Transmission fluid type: ________________________**
   c. **Transmission fluid capacity: ________________ qt/lt**
   d. **Pan bolts torque: ________________ in-lb/ft-lb/N·m**
   e. **Filter screw torque, if needed: ________________ in-lb/ft-lb/N·m**
   f. **List the steps required to properly check the fluid level:**

2. **Following the specified procedure, remove the transmission pan and filter (filter may be an external filter). Inspect any residue and debris in the bottom of the pan or stuck to the filter. List your observations:**

3. **Determine any necessary action(s):**

4. **Have your supervisor/instructor verify removal of the pan and filter. Supervisor's/instructor's initials: ____________**

5. **Clean the pan, magnet, and gasket surfaces.**

6. **Following the specified procedure, install the filter, pan, gasket, initial amount of fluid, and any other removed components.**

> NOTE Make sure you fill the transmission with the proper amount of the specified fluid. Most service information lists two fluid capacities: one for a drain and refill, and the second for an overhaul. Make sure you use the proper specification.

7. **Follow the specified procedure to circulate the fluid and bleed any air from the system. This usually involves moving the gear selector through each position and then checking the fluid level. Add fluid to bring the fluid to the proper level (do NOT overfill).**

8. **Verify the correct operation of the transmission. This may require a test drive. Get your supervisor's/instructor's permission before performing this step, and list your observation(s):**

9. **Have your supervisor/instructor verify satisfactory completion of this procedure, any observations found, and any necessary action(s) recommended.**

Performance Rating

CDX Tasksheet Number: C907

☐	☐	☐	☐	☐
0	1	2	3	4

Supervisor/instructor signature ______________________ Date ________

▶ TASK Identify and interpret transmission/transaxle concerns, differentiate between engine performance and transmission/transaxle concerns; determine needed action.

MAST 2A1

Time off__________

Time on__________

Total time__________

CDX Tasksheet Number: C599

1. **Ask your instructor to assign you a vehicle that has a potential transmission/engine performance concern. List the customer concern(s):**

2. **Research the particular concern in the appropriate service manual.**
   a. **List the possible causes:**

3. **Inspect the vehicle to determine the cause of the concern (differentiate between engine performance and transmission/transaxle concerns).**
   a. **List the steps you took and their results to determine the fault(s):**

4. **List the cause of the concern(s):**

5. **List the necessary action(s) to correct the fault(s):**

6. **Have your supervisor/instructor verify satisfactory completion of this procedure, any observations found, and any necessary action(s) recommended.**

Performance Rating

CDX Tasksheet Number: C599

☐	☐	☐	☐	☐
0	1	2	3	4

Supervisor/instructor signature ____________________ Date __________

▶ TASK Diagnose noise and vibration concerns; determine needed action.

MAST 2A7

Time off________

Time on________

Total time________

CDX Tasksheet Number: C743

Vehicle used for this activity:

Year ________ Make ________ Model________

Odometer________ VIN________

1. **List the transmission-noise and vibration-related concern:**

2. **Research the concern in the appropriate service information.**
   a. **List the possible cause(s) of the concern:**

   b. **List or print off and attach to this sheet the specified procedure for diagnosing the concern:**

3. **Perform the appropriate tests, following the specified procedure. List your observation(s):**

4. **List the cause(s) of the concern:**

5. **Determine any necessary action(s) to correct the fault:**

6. **Have your supervisor/instructor verify satisfactory completion of this procedure, any observations found, and any necessary action(s) recommended.**

Performance Rating

CDX Tasksheet Number: C743

0	1	2	3	4
☐	☐	☐	☐	☐

Supervisor/instructor signature ______________________________ Date ____________

▶ TASK Diagnose electronic transmission/transaxle control systems using appropriate test equipment and service information.

MAST 2A11

Time off________

Time on________

Total time________

CDX Tasksheet Number: C600

1. **List the customer concern related to an electronic control system issue:**

2. **Connect an appropriate scan tool to the data link connector (DLC). Retrieve and list any transmission-related codes:**

3. **Research the specifications and procedures for diagnosing the code(s).**
    a. **List the possible cause(s) of the code(s):**

    b. **List or print off and attach to this sheet the procedure for diagnosing the code(s):**

4. **Perform the diagnostic tests following the specified procedure using the appropriate test equipment.**
    a. **List your tests and test results:**

b. List the test equipment you used to diagnose this concern:

5. Determine any necessary action(s) to correct the fault:

6. Have your supervisor/instructor verify satisfactory completion of this procedure, any observations found, and any necessary action(s) recommended.

Performance Rating

CDX Tasksheet Number: C600

0	1	2	3	4
☐	☐	☐	☐	☐

Supervisor/instructor signature ____________________ Date __________

▶ TASK Inspect, test, adjust, repair, and/or replace electrical/electronic components and circuits, including computers, solenoids, sensors, relays, terminals, connectors, switches, and harnesses; demonstrate understanding of relearn procedure.

MAST 2B3

Time off__________

Time on__________

Total time__________

CDX Tasksheet Number: C601

1. **Research the specifications and procedures for inspecting, testing, adjusting, and replacing the electrical/electronic components and sensors.**
   a. **List or print off and attach to this sheet the procedure for inspecting, testing, adjusting, and replacing these components:**

   b. **List any specified precautions:**

2. **Inspect the following components for proper operation and list your observations.**
   a. **Computer:**

   b. **Solenoids/relays:**

   c. **Sensors/switches:**

   d. **Terminals/connectors/harnesses:**

3. **Ask your instructor which components you should replace.**
   a. **Computer: Yes: __________ No: __________**
   b. **Solenoids/relays: Yes: __________ No: __________**
   c. **Sensors/switches: Yes: __________ No: __________**
   d. **Terminals/connectors/harnesses: Yes: __________ No: __________**

4. Remove the appropriate component(s) following the specified procedure. List your observation(s):

5. Have your supervisor/instructor verify removal and your observations. Supervisor's/instructor's initials: ____________

6. Replace each component following the specified procedure.

7. Adjust each component following the specified procedure.

8. Have your supervisor/instructor verify satisfactory completion of this procedure, any observations found, and any necessary action(s) recommended.

Performance Rating

CDX Tasksheet Number: C601

☐	☐	☐	☐	☐
0	1	2	3	4

Supervisor/instructor signature ______________________________ Date __________

▶ TASK Perform stall test; determine needed action.

MAST 2A8

Time off________

Time on________

Total time________

CDX Tasksheet Number: C741

1. **Research the specifications and procedures to stall test this transmission.**

> **NOTE** Do not perform this test on a transmission if the line pressure is not up to specifications or further damage to the transmission could quickly result. Also, some manufacturers do not want their transmissions stall tested. And on vehicles with electronic throttle control, the PCM may not allow a stall test to be performed without a scan tool.

   a. **Does the manufacturer recommend a stall test? Yes: _______ No: _______**
   b. **Specified stall speed(s) ________________________________**
   c. **List all precautions when performing the stall test:**

2. **Perform the stall test. Be sure to follow all safety precautions. List your observation(s):**

3. **Determine any necessary action(s):**

4. **Have your supervisor/instructor verify satisfactory completion of this procedure, any observations found, and any necessary action(s) recommended.**

Performance Rating

CDX Tasksheet Number: C741

☐	☐	☐	☐	☐
0	1	2	3	4

Supervisor/instructor signature ________________________________ Date ____________

▶ TASK Perform pressure tests (including transmissions/transaxles equipped with electronic pressure control); determine needed action.

MAST 2A6

Time off________

Time on________

Total time________

CDX Tasksheet Number: C740

1. **Research all applicable pressure specifications and test procedure(s) for this transmission in the appropriate service information.**
    a. **Line pressure: ____________________ psi/kPa**
    b. **Governor pressure: ____________________ psi/kPa**
    c. **Throttle pressure: ____________________ psi/kPa**
    d. **Low-gear servo/clutch pressure: ____________________ psi/kPa**
    e. **Second-gear servo/clutch pressure: ____________________ psi/kPa**
    f. **Direct-clutch pressure: ____________________ psi/kPa**
    g. **Cooler-circuit pressure: ____________________ psi/kPa**
    h. **List any other pressure specifications off to the right side of the above specifications.**

2. **Perform the applicable transmission-pressure tests. Be sure to follow the specified procedures. Note that a scan tool may need to be used on electronically controlled transmissions. List your observations below.**
    a. **Line pressure: ____________________ psi/kPa**
    b. **Governor pressure: ____________________ psi/kPa**
    c. **Throttle pressure: ____________________ psi/kPa**
    d. **Low-gear servo/clutch pressure: ____________________ psi/kPa**
    e. **Second-gear servo/clutch pressure: ____________________ psi/kPa**
    f. **Direct-clutch pressure: ____________________ psi/kPa**
    g. **Cooler-circuit pressure: ____________________ psi/kPa**
    h. **List any other pressures off to the right side of the above readings.**

3. **Determine any necessary action(s):**

4. **Have your supervisor/instructor verify satisfactory completion of this procedure, any observations found, and any necessary action(s) recommended.**

Performance Rating

CDX Tasksheet Number: C740

0	1	2	3	4

Supervisor/instructor signature ____________________ Date ________

▶ TASK Inspect for leakage; replace external seals, gaskets, and bushings.

MAST 2B2

Time off________

Time on________

Total time________

CDX Tasksheet Number: C748

Vehicle used for this activity:

Year ____________ Make ________________________ Model ________________________

Odometer ____________________ VIN ____

1. **Safely raise and support the vehicle on a hoist.**
2. **Inspect the transmission/transaxle seals and gaskets for leaks.**
    a. **List each external seal, gasket, and bushing; and identify the source of any leak(s):**
3. **With your instructor's permission, replace any leaking seals or gaskets. List the parts replaced and your observations:**
4. **Have your supervisor/instructor verify satisfactory completion of this procedure, any observations found, and any necessary action(s) recommended.**

Performance Rating

CDX Tasksheet Number: C748

☐	☐	☐	☐	☐
0	1	2	3	4

Supervisor/instructor signature ________________________________ Date ____________

▶ TASK Inspect, replace, and/or align powertrain mounts.

MAST 2B5

Time off________

Time on________

Total time________

CDX Tasksheet Number: C602

Vehicle used for this activity:

Year______________ Make ______________________________ Model______________________

Odometer____________________________ VIN ____

1. **Research the procedure to inspect, replace, and align the powertrain mounts in the appropriate service information.**
   a. **List the type of mount(s) this vehicle uses:** ______________________________
   b. **List or print off and attach to this sheet the procedure for inspecting the mount(s):**
   c. **List or print off and attach to this sheet the precautions for performing this task:**
2. **Following the specified procedure, inspect each of the powertrain mounts, and list your observations:**
3. **Determine any necessary action(s):**
4. **Have your supervisor/instructor verify your answers. Supervisor's/instructor's initials:** ______________________________
5. **With your supervisor/instructor's permission, remove one or more powertrain mounts following the specified procedure. Inspect the removed mount(s) and list your observations:**

6. **Have your supervisor/instructor verify the removal of the mount. Supervisor's/instructor's initials: ____________**

7. **Reinstall and align the powertrain mount(s) according to the specified procedure.**

8. **Determine any necessary action(s):**

9. **Have your supervisor/instructor verify satisfactory completion of this procedure, any observations found, and any necessary action(s) recommended.**

Performance Rating

CDX Tasksheet Number: C602

0	1	2	3	4
☐	☐	☐	☐	☐

Supervisor/instructor signature ____________ Date ____________

▶ TASK Perform lock-up converter system tests; determine needed action.

MAST 2A9

Time off________

Time on________

Total time________

CDX Tasksheet Number: C063

1. **Research the specifications and procedure for testing the lock-up converter.**
   a. **Lock-up converter solenoid resistance: ____________ ohms**
   b. **List or print off and attach to this sheet the procedure for testing the lock-up converter:**
   c. **Ask your instructor where you are to perform the lock-up converter test: Road test: ________ Vehicle hoist: ________**
2. **Have your supervisor/instructor approve your answers. Supervisor's/instructor's initials: ____________**
3. **Perform the lock-up converter performance test.**
   a. **Prepare the vehicle for this test by following the specified procedure.**
   b. **Test the operation of the lock-up converter system following your instructor's directions. List your observation(s):**
4. **Perform the lock-up converter pinpoint test.**
   a. **Test for the proper electrical signal at the lock-up converter solenoid connector following the specified procedure. List your observation(s):**
   b. **Measure the electrical continuity/resistance of the solenoid: ________ ohms**
5. **Determine any necessary action(s):**

6. **Have your supervisor/instructor verify satisfactory completion of this procedure, any observations found, and any necessary action(s) recommended.**

Performance Rating

CDX Tasksheet Number: C063

☐	☐	☐	☐	☐
0	1	2	3	4

Supervisor/instructor signature _______________ Date _______

▶ TASK Inspect, adjust, and/or replace manual-valve shift linkage, transmission-range sensor/switch, and park/neutral position switch.

MAST
2B1

Time off________

Time on________

Total time________

CDX Tasksheet Number: C683

1. **Research the specifications and procedures for inspecting, adjusting, and replacing the manual valve shift linkage, transmission range sensor/switch, and park/neutral position switch in the appropriate service information.**
   a. **List or print off and attach to this sheet the procedure for inspecting, adjusting, and replacing these components:**

   b. **List any specified precautions:**

2. **Inspect the following components for proper operation. List your observations.**
   a. **Manual-valve shift linkage:**

   b. **Transmission-range sensor/switch:**

   c. **Park/neutral position switch:**

3. **Ask your instructor which components you should replace.**
   a. **Manual valve shift linkage: Yes: ________ No: ________**
   b. **Transmission-range sensor/switch: Yes: ________ No: ________**
   c. **Park/neutral position switch: Yes: ________ No: ________**

4. **Remove the appropriate component(s) following the specified procedure. List your observation(s):**

5. **Have your supervisor/instructor verify removal. Supervisor's/instructor's initials: ____________________**

6. **Replace each component following the specified procedure.**

7. **Adjust each component following the specified procedure.**

8. **Have your supervisor/instructor verify satisfactory completion of this procedure, any observations found, and any necessary action(s) recommended.**

Performance Rating

CDX Tasksheet Number: C683

0	1	2	3	4

Supervisor/instructor signature ________________________________ Date __________

▶ TASK Describe the operational characteristics of a hybrid vehicle drive train.

MAST 2C5

Time off________

Time on________

Total time________

CDX Tasksheet Number: C607

1. **Research the description and operation of a hybrid vehicle drive train in the appropriate service information.**
    a. **What type of hybrid is this vehicle?**
       Series: ____________ **Parallel:** ____________ **Series-Parallel:** ____________
    b. **Can this vehicle operate only on the internal combustion engine?**
       Yes: __________ **No:** __________
    c. **Describe the conditions when the internal combustion engine runs:**
    d. **Can this vehicle operate only on the electric motor?**
       Yes: ________ **No:** ________
    e. **Describe the conditions when the electric motor operates:**
    f. **Does this vehicle use regeneration?**
       Yes: ________ **No:** ________
    g. **Describe how regeneration operates in this vehicle:**
2. **Have your supervisor/instructor verify satisfactory completion of this procedure, any observations found, and any necessary action(s) recommended.**

Performance Rating

CDX Tasksheet Number: C607

0	1	2	3	4
☐	☐	☐	☐	☐

Supervisor/instructor signature ______________________________ Date ____________

▶ TASK Describe the operational characteristics of a continuously variable transmission (CVT).

MAST 2C4

Time off________

Time on________

Total time________

CDX Tasksheet Number: C606

Vehicle used for this activity:

Year____________ Make________________________ Model________________

Odometer____________________ VIN ______________________________

1. **Research the description and operation of a continuously variable transmission in the appropriate service information.**
   a. **What type of CVT is this transmission?**____________________
   b. **How does this CVT achieve reduction?**
   c. **How does this CVT achieve direct drive?**
   d. **How does this CVT achieve neutral?**
   e. **How does this CVT achieve reverse?**

f. **What type of fluid does this CVT use?** ______________________________

g. **What is the fluid capacity?** ______________________ **qt/lt**

h. **What is the service interval for the transmission fluid?** __________ **mi/km**

i. **Look up if there is a fluid condition monitor for the transmission. What is the procedure to reset the fluid monitor?**

2. **Have your supervisor/instructor verify satisfactory completion of this procedure, any observations found, and any necessary action(s) recommended.**

Performance Rating

CDX Tasksheet Number: C606

0	1	2	3	4
☐	☐	☐	☐	☐

Supervisor/instructor signature ______________________________ Date __________

Appendix: CDX/NATEF Correlation Guide

Section AT 211: Suspension and Steering Systems

CDX Tasksheet Number	2017 MAST NATEF Reference and Priority	Corresponding Page(s)
C166	4A1; P-1	1-2
C851	4A2; P-1	3
NN04	N/A	5-6
C619	4F1; P-1	7-8
C222	4F3; P-1	9-10
C620	4F6; P-1	11-12
C936	4F11: P-1	13-14
C621	4F7; P-1	15-17
C855	4F2; P-2	19-20
C796	4F5; P-1	21-22
C580	4F8; P-1	23-24
C552	4F9; P-1	25
C701	4F4; P-2	27-28
C937	4F10; P-1	29-30
C931	4D3; P-3	31
C551	4B19; P-2	33
C179	4B11; P-1	35
C884	4B4; P-2	37-38
C880	4B5; P-2	39-40
C170	4B3; P-2	41-42
C177	4B9; P-1	43
C178	4B10; P-2	45
C180	4B12; P-1	47-48
C181	4B13; P-2	49
C699	4B14; P-2	51
C183	4B15; P-2	53

CDX Tasksheet Number	2017 MAST NATEF Reference number and Priority	Corresponding Page(s)
C1001	4B20; P-2	55
C882	4B7; P-2	57-58
C883	4B8; P-1	59
C184	4B16; P-2	61-63
C185	4B17; P-1	65-66
C186	4B18; P-2	67-68
C464	0A13; P-1	69-70
C168	4B1; P-1	71-72
C169	4B2; P-1	73
C173	4B6; P-2	75-76
C852	4C1; P-1	77-78
C853	4C2; P-1	79-80
C206	4E1; P-1	81-82
C793	4C9; P-3	83-84
C202	4D1; P-1	85-86
C193	4C7; P-3	87-88
C192	4C6; P-3	89
C790	4C3; P-3	91-92
C791	4C4; P-3	93
C792	4C5; P-2	95-96
C794	4C10; P-3	97-98
C854	4C12; P-1	99-100
C203	4D2; P-1	101-102
C934	4C11; P-3	103-104
C194	4C8; P-3	105-106
C617	4E2; P-1	107-108
C618	4E3; P-1	109
C940	4E9; P-2	111
C213	4E4; P-2	113
C214	4E5; P-2	115
C216	4E6; P-1	117
C217	4E7; P-2	119-120
C795	4E8; P-3	121

Section AT 110: Brakes		
CDX Tasksheet Number	2017 MAST NATEF Reference and Priority	Corresponding Page(s)
C230	5A2; P-1	123
NN05	N/A	125-126
C950	5G2; P-3	127
C706	5C1; P-1	129-130
C251	5A4; P-1	131
C800	5C2; P-1	133-134
C626	5C3; P-1	135
C248	5C4; P-1	137-138
C707	5C5; P-2	139-140
C801	5C6; P-1	141-142
C229	5A1; P-1	143
C944	5A3; P-1	145
C708	5D1; P-1	147-148
C236	5B5; P-1	149-150
C802	5D2; P-1	151
C803	5D3; P-1	153
C632	5D11; P-1	155
C627	5D4; P-1	157
C805	5D5; P-1	159
C631	5D10; P-2	161
C251	5A4; P-1	163
C628	5D6; P-1	165
C806	5D7; P-1	167
C629	5D8; P-1	169
C630	5D9; P-1	171
C274	5F8; P-1	173-174
C948	5D12; P-1	175
C808	5E2; P-1	177
C239	5B9; P-1	179
C625	5B13; P-1	181
C705	5B12; P-1	183
C622	5B2; P-1	185-186
C807	5E1; P-2	187-188
C894	5B1; P-1	189
C704	5B3; P-1	191-192
C235	5B4; P-1	193
C556	5E5; P-3	195
C809	5E3; P-1	197-198

CDX Tasksheet Number	2017 MAST NATEF Reference number and Priority	Corresponding Page(s)
C581	5E4; P-3	199-200
C237	5B6; P-1	201
C623	5B7; P-2	203
C624	5B8; P-2	205
C947	5B11; P-2	207
C242	5B10; P-3	209
C633	5F4; P-1	211
C811	5F3; P-1	213
C272	5F5; P-1	215
C267	5F1; P-1	217-218
C810	5F2; P-2	219-220
C273	5F6; P-3	221-222
C275	5F7; P-1	223
C134	3D3; P-1	225-226
C637	5G6; P-1	227
C812	5G5; P-2	229
C635	5G3; P-2	231
C636	5G4; P-2	233-234
C634	5G1; P-1	235
C639	5G7; P-2	237
C813	5G8; P-1	239

Section AT 106: Manual Drive Train and Axles		
CDX Tasksheet Number	2017 MAST NATEF Reference and Priority	Corresponding Page(s)
C102	3A2; P-1	241
C101	3A1; P-1	243
NN03	N/A	245-246
C107	3B2; P-1	247-248
C938	3B5; P-1	249
C111	3B4; P-1	251-252
C106	3B1; P-1	253-254
C847	3B6; P-1	255
C848	3B7; P-2	257
C608	3B3; P-1	259-260
C611	3C2; P-2	261
C691	3A3; P-1	263
C105	3A4; P-1	265

CDX Tasksheet Number	2017 MAST NATEF Reference and Priority	Corresponding Page(s)
C609	3C3; P-2	267
C693	3C4; P-2	269
C887	3C5; P-3	271
C910	3C6; P-2	273
C768	3C1; P-2	275-276
C691	3A3; P-1	277
C911	3E1:2; P-1	279
C912	3E1:3; P-1	281
C779	3D5; P-2	283-284
C133	3D2; P-2	285-286
C850	3E3:4; P-2	287
C155	3E3:2; P-1	289
C156	3E3:3; P-2	291-292
C849	3D4; P-1	293-294
C134	3D3; P-1	295-296
C138	3E1:4; P-2	297
C153	3E3:5; P-2	299-300
C154	3E3:1; P-1	301-302
C784	3E2:1; P-3	303
C132	3D1; P-1	305-306
C889	3E1:5; P-2	307-308
C780	3E1:6; P-3	309
C890	3E1:7; P-3	311-312
C147	3E1:12; P-3	313-314
C781	3E1:8; P-3	315
C782	3E1:9; P-3	317
C148	3E1:13; P-3	319
C145	3E1:10; P-3	321
C783	3E1:11; P-3	323
C785	3E1:1; P-1	325-326
C786	3E2:2; P-3	327
C787	3F5; P-3	329-330
C613	3F4; P-2	331
C878	3F6; P-2	333
C788	3F1; P-3	335-336
C914	3F3; P-3	337-338
C875	3F7; P-2	339-340
C876	3F2; P-3	341-342

Section AT 207: Automatic Transmission and Transaxle		
CDX Tasksheet Number	2017 MAST NATEF Reference and Priority	Corresponding Page(s)
C681	2A2; P-1	343
NN02	N/A	345-346
C747	2A12; P-2	347-348
C066	2A10; P-1	349-350
C604	2C1; P-2	351-353
C605	2C3; P-2	355-356
C749	2C2; P-1	357
C689	2C11; P-1	359
C684	2C6; P-1	361-362
C688	2C10; P-2	363-364
C752	2C15; P-2	365
C751	2C14; P-2	367
C750	2C12; P-2	369
C759	2C22; P-2	371
C690	2C13; P-2	373
C753	2C16; P-2	375
C756	2C19; P-2	377-378
C757	2C20; P-1	379
C758	2C21; P-1	381-382
C686	2C8; P-2	383
C685	2C7; P-2	385-386
C755	2C18; P-2	387-388
C754	2C17; P-2	389-390
C083	2C9; P-1	391-392
C902	2A4; P-1	393
C903X	2A5; P-1	395
C682	2A3; P-1	397
C907	2B4; P-1	399-400
C599	2A1; P-1	401-402
C743	2A7; P-2	403-404
C600	2A11; P-1	405-406
C601	2B3; P-1	407-408
C741	2A8; P-2	409
C740	2A6; P-1	411
C748	2B2; P-2	413
C602	2B5; P-2	415-416

CDX Tasksheet Number	2017 MAST NATEF Reference and Priority	Corresponding Page(s)
C063	2A9; P-3	417-418
C683	2B1; P-1	419-420
C607	2C5; P-3	421
C606	2C4; P-3	423-424